New York City in the 1980s:
A Social, Economic, and Political Atlas

New York City in the 1980s: A Social, Economic, and Political Atlas

John H. Mollenkopf

SIMON & SCHUSTER

A Paramount Communications Company

New York   London   Toronto   Sydney   Tokyo   Singapore

Library of Congress Cataloging-in-Publication Data

Mollenkopf. John H., 1946–
    New York City in the 1980's: a social, economic, and political
    atlas / John H. Mollenkopf.
        p.   cm.
    Includes bibliographical references and index.
    ISBN 0–13–616293–2
        1. New York (N.Y.)—Social conditions—Maps.   2. New York (N.Y.)—
Economic conditions—Maps.   3. New York (N.Y.)—Population—Maps.
4. New York (N.Y.)—Politics and government—Maps.   I. Title.
G1254.N4E1M6   1993   <G&M>
912.747'1—dc20   93-25096
                                CIP
                              MAP

Table of Contents

Note to the Reader

This atlas maps the rapidly changing social, economic, and political climate in New York City during the 1980s. It shows how economic and demographic change affected the New York City landscape and consequently the political and social climate of the city.

There are three main sections: Race, Income, and Immigration; Social Problems and Community Resources; and Political Participation. Each section is accompanied by maps, charts, and tables that depict patterns and trends. The *Atlas* concludes with appendix tables, bibliography, and index.

The *Atlas* features a series of 59 full-color maps supported by 1980 and 1990 Census information, New York City Board of Elections' returns, and other government information. Each map is numbered, referenced at an appropriate point in the text, and includes a legend box describing information measured by dollars, groups, numbers, percent, percentage points, or some other unit.

The maps in Section I are based on information found in the Standard Tape File 4 (STF4) of the 1980 Census and the STF3 of the 1990 Census. The black-and-white map on page viii shows the city's 2,200 Census tracts as of 1980 onto which the Census data were mapped. Each tract represents approximately 3,300 people. Section I shows where whites, blacks, Latinos, and Asians lived in New York City in 1990 and how their demographic and economic status has changed since 1980.

Section II examines the trends in the economic and demographic changes in the population between 1980 and 1990 and addresses their social ramifications, such as the unequal distribution of incomes, jobs, poverty, and health. The maps of community organizations are drawn from a census by the Nonprofit Coordinating Committee of New York and the Fund for the City of New York and are mapped by Census tracts. Health and mortality statistics obtained from the New York City Department of Health are mapped according to 176 residential zip codes.

Section III explains the role that various groups played in supporting candidates for city elections and their influence on determining the election outcomes. The maps in this section use the boundaries of the 60 Assembly Districts (ADs) that existed between 1982 and 1992. (See p. ix.) ADs are the primary units of organization for political parties in New York State.

NEW YORK CITY'S 2,200 CENSUS TRACTS
EACH TRACT CONTAINS ABOUT 3,300 PEOPLE

Van Cortland Park

BRONX

Rikers Island

MANHATTAN

La Guardia Airport

Central Park

Prospect Park

Flushing Meadows

BROOKLYN

Kennedy Airport

Coney Island

QUEENS

STATEN ISLAND

ABBREVIATIONS USED IN THIS ATLAS

AD	Assembly District
AFDC	Aid to Families with Dependent Children
DCP	Department of City Planning
HPD	Housing Preservation and Development Department
PUMS	Public Use Microdata Sample
STF	Standard Tape File

Neighborhoods Covered by Assembly Districts (ADs; 1982–1992 Boundaries)

QUEENS
23 Rockaways, Rosedale
24 Fresh Meadows
25 Bayside, Bellerose
26 Whitestone
27 Flushing, Briarwood
28 Forest Hills, Kew Gardens
29 St. Albans, Cambria Heights
30 Elmhurst, Rego Park
31 Richmond Hill, Ozone Park
32 Rochdale Village
33 Queens Village, South Jamaica
34 Jackson Heights
35 Corona, East Elmhurst
36 Astoria, Long Island City
37 Sunnyside, Ridgewood
38 Woodhaven, Middle Village

BROOKLYN
39 Canarsie, Mill Basin
40 Brownsville, East New York
41 Flatlands, Sheepshead Bay
42 Midwood
43 Crown Heights, Flatbush
44 Flatbush, Park Slope
45 Midwood, Manhattan Beach
46 Coney Island, Brighton
47 Gravesend, Bensonhurst
48 Borough Park, Dyker Heights
49 Bensonhurst, Bath Beach
50 Greenpoint, Williamsburg
51 Park Slope, Sunset Park
52 Brooklyn Heights, Carroll Gardens
53 Bushwick, Williamsburgh
54 Bushwick, Cyprus Hills
55 Ocean Hill, Brownsville
56 Bedford-Stuyvesant
57 Fort Greene, Prospect Heights

STATEN ISLAND
58 North Shore
59 Mid-Island
60 South Shore

MANHATTAN
61 Greenwich Village, Downtown
62 Lower East Side, Chinatown
63 Stuyvesant Town
64 Chelsea, Central Park West
65 Yorkville, Roosevelt Island
66 Upper East Side
67 Upper West Side
68 East Harlem
69 Morningside Heights
70 Central Harlem
71 Washington Heights
72 Inwood, Marble Hill

BRONX
73 South Bronx, Hunts Point
74 Soundview, Bronx River
75 Parkchester, Throgs Neck
76 Highbridge, Morris Heights
77 University Heights, Fordham
78 Morrisania, East Tremont
79 Bedford Park, Belmont
80 Riverdale, Woodlawn
81 Pelham Parkway, Co-Op City
82 Williamsbridge, Baychester

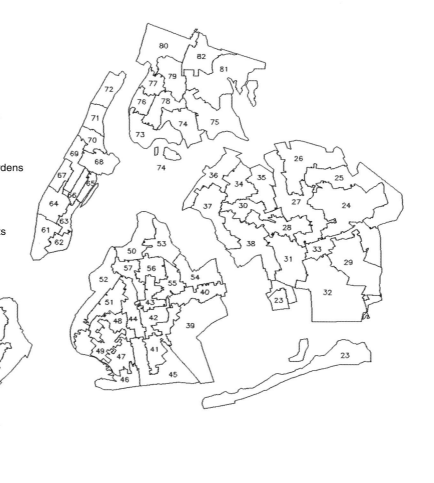

ACKNOWLEDGMENTS

The data used in this *Atlas* were assembled by the author and his associates from a variety of sources. Ms. Marta Fisch of the CUNY Data Service did a superb job in developing information from the 1980 and 1990 Censuses. Without her efforts, this publication simply would not have been possible. Lorraine Minnite and Kimberly Johnson gathered additional information from a variety of official sources. Ms. Minnite tracked down and coded registration and voting data from the NYC Board of Elections used in the analysis presented in the third section. Ms. Johnson gathered data from other official sources and did a virtuoso job developing prototypes for most of the maps used here. While any remaining errors are my responsibility, I would particularly like to acknowledge that the strengths of this *Atlas* owe much to the excellent work of Ms. Fisch and Ms. Johnson. Thanks are also due Princeton University Press for permission to reproduce Tables 2–4 and Appendix Tables 1 and 2 from *A Phoenix in the Ashes*.

Over time, many people have provided information sources essential to the *Atlas* or valuable advice about how to develop it. Bruce Posner and Barbara Rubinstein of the Fund for the City of New York provided boundary files, data, and extensive advice. Len Rodberg of the Queens College Urban Studies Program and Mark Eichen of Academic Computing at Hunter College offered frequent help with boundary files and programming issues. John Freed, database editor of *The New York Times,* also provided much-needed assistance. Terry Rosenberg of the Community Service Society shared many thoughts gained from her own extensive experience in mapping social indicators for New York City and reviewed the manuscript.

Alan Gartner and Herman Jenkins provided me with a chance to delve deeply into political geography as a consultant to the New York City Districting Commission. My great thanks go to them and to my map-drawing colleagues. Mark Lapidus, Kevin McCabe, and Phil Thompson were especially helpful, sharing their special knowledge about the electoral geography of various parts of the city.

All those who map data in New York City, myself included, are indebted to Jack Eichenbaum for his leadership, with Bruce Posner, of GISMO, an organization designed to share information and assistance among those in city government and elsewhere who use desktop mapping in their work. Art Blank of the United Hospital Fund, Al Leidner of the Department of Environmental Protection, and William James of the Police Department all provided important files and advised me about their respective areas of expertise. As part of a collaborative project with the CUNY Graduate Center, the Information Systems Division of the New York City Department of City Planning (DCP) also made a number of official boundary files available. My thanks go to Linda Goldsmith, Rich Steinberg, and Mike Miller for their help at various points. Joe Salvo of DCP's population unit provided data on immigration to New York City and allowed me to draw on his fount of knowledge on the subject.

CUNY Chancellor W. Ann Reynolds and President Frances Degen Horowitz of the CUNY Graduate Center encouraged this effort at crucial times and sought to strengthen the ways in which research done at CUNY can help the city to address and resolve its vexing problems. This project was sponsored by and received financial support from the Robert Wagner, Sr., Institute of Urban Public Policy of the City University of New York. The Institute was established at the Graduate School and University Center in 1987 by Joseph S. Murphy, University Professor of Political Science and CUNY Chancellor from 1982 to 1990. Professor Asher Arian, director of the Institute, provided unfailing support and guidance, as did Donald Glickman, Wagner Project Administrator.

The data were mapped using Atlas*GIS software. When Strategic Mapping, Inc., could not tell me how its DOS-based program could write output files that could be input to the MAC-based equipment used by M. E. Aslett Corporation, producer of the color separations for the *Atlas*, it referred me to mapping consultant Stuart Shydlow, who suggested using HiJaak to convert screen capture files into MAC TIFF files. With assistance from Patrick Gorman of M. E. Aslett Corporation, this solution ultimately worked.

The Social Science Research Council and its president, Dr. David Featherman, provided an exciting and supportive environment for the completion of this work. He, too, is strongly committed to promoting efforts by scholars to better understand the difficult urban problems described in the *Atlas* and to communicate with policymakers to make that knowledge more useful. Charles E. Smith, President of Simon and Schuster's Academic Reference Division, believed in the value of this *Atlas* and showed great patience while we cut through the obstacles in its way. He is everything that an author could ask for in his or her editor. Michael Aslett and Kathryn Bleckman also did a superb job of realizing the end product.

Finally, my wife Kathleen Gerson and daughter Emily Gerson Mollenkopf have supported my work, tolerated my newfound fascination with making maps, and kept me from taking myself too seriously. My debt to them both is profound. It is a pleasure to dedicate this book to Emily, who delights her parents with her eagerness to explore and understand the world around her.

INTRODUCTION

Most people who lived in New York City during the 1980s saw the rapid changes that took place in who lived in the city, how they got along with one another, what jobs they held, who got ahead and who did not, and what was happening to the neighborhoods in which they lived. These changes coincided with ferment in the city's political system and they challenged its capacity to innovate. Important questions arose for neighborhood residents, workers in community organizations and in government agencies, and specialists on urban problems alike: Which groups were growing and which were declining in the city? Where did they live? What jobs did they have and what was happening to their incomes? What kinds of problems were facing their neighborhoods? Finally, who participated in the city's electoral politics and how were they voting?

New York City in the 1980s: A Social, Economic, and Political Atlas maps the answers to such questions. By offering a comprehensive view of these issues, drawing on detailed information from the 1980 and 1990 U.S. Censuses and other official sources, the *Atlas* shows how economic and demographic change altered the face of New York City and highlights some of the social and political consequences. It tells the story of the declining population descended from last century's immigrants, the growing population of native-born African Americans and Puerto Ricans, and the newly arrived wave of immigrants and how they have intersected with the city's changing economic structure to produce new patterns in the social, economic,

and political geography of the city. The *Atlas* also traces the consequences of the growth of corporate and social services and the decay of manufacturing as well as their effects on the old ethnic and racial groups and the new immigrants. Further, it shows where immigrants from the Caribbean, Latin America, and Asia have chosen to settle in relation to the areas where native-born white ethnics, blacks, and Puerto Ricans have previously settled.[1] It then examines the political consequences of these changes in detail.

The *Atlas* has three sections. Each presents and discusses a series of maps accompanied by charts and tables. The first section, "Race, Income, and Immigration," describes where whites, blacks, Latinos, and Asians lived in New York City in 1990, how each group's pattern of settlement has changed since 1980, and how income is distributed across each group. It then explores where native-born and immigrant ethnic groups that make up each racial category live in relationship to each

---

[1] On the U.S. Census Bureau forms, a person can designate his or her race as white, black, Asian, American Indian, or other, but not Hispanic. Hispanic persons can be of any race, but they grow up in a Spanish-speaking culture. In 1990, most Hispanics said they were either "white" or "other." Race and Hispanic origin can be used to define mutually exclusive groups of non-Hispanic whites, blacks, Asians, American Indians, others, and all Hispanics. Unless otherwise noted, all subsequent references to whites, blacks, and Asians exclude Hispanics, who are grouped together and termed Latino. The Census also asked a sample of individuals their ancestry, although only half reported one. Native-born whites of Russian, Polish, Irish, Italian, and German ancestry are termed white ethnics. Those of Russian, Polish, and Hungarian ancestry are most likely to be Jewish, although these ancestries are only a rough proxy for religious background.

other. These maps rely on Standard Tape File 4 (STF4) of the 1980 Census and STF3 of the 1990 Census, grouped according to the city's 2,200 Census tracts as of 1980. The average tract contains about 3,300 people.

Section II, "Social Problems and Community Resources," relates these broader trends in the population and the economy to social issues like labor force participation, the unequal distribution of income, poverty, and health outcomes. This section also uses homicides as an indicator of the quality of neighborhood life. Finally, it shows where low- and moderate-income housing has been constructed and where social service organizations and religious groups are located. These two last two indicators are drawn from a census undertaken by the Nonprofit Coordinating Committee of New York with the assistance of the Fund for the City of New York. Other data in this section are drawn from Census sources and are mapped by Census tracts. Health and mortality statistics come from the New York City Department of Health and are mapped according to 176 residential zip codes.

The final section, "Political Participation," examines how different groups have mobilized in city elections during the 1980s and what effect they have had on who won elections. This section uses the 60 Assembly Districts (ADs) that existed between 1982 and 1992. It maps changing patterns of party registration, turnout, and candidate preference for the most important citywide Democratic primary and general elections between 1982 and 1991. It emphasizes the historic 1989 race in which the city elected its first African-American mayor.

Section I

Race, Income, and Immigration

Change is a constant in New York. Between 1848 and the 1880s, almost one million Irish and German immigrants arrived in New York and Brooklyn. From the turn of the century until the nation closed its borders to new immigrants in 1919, one million more Central European Jews and one-half million Italians joined them. In those same years, a small number of African Americans began to migrate north to the city, and their numbers swelled during and after World War II. Puerto Rican migrants also arrived in large numbers in the 1950s and 1960s.

New York's economy was also rapidly evolving. New York City began as a port city and trading center in the early nineteenth century, became a manufacturing center in the late nineteenth and early twentieth centuries, and ultimately evolved into a postindustrial center for global business activities. The question of how today's immigrants are finding work in this new economic structure thus echoes changes that took place a century ago, when the parents and grandparents of those who are now seen as the establishment were new immigrants themselves.

Although change is a constant, the city evolved in some new and unexpected directions during the 1980s. From the 1950s through the 1970s, white ethnic residents and goods-related jobs moved to the suburbs, the city's population declined and became more black and Latino, and the city's economy declined relative to the region and the nation. The severe recessions of the early 1970s and the subsequent fiscal crisis accelerated these trends. Most people expected these trends to continue into the 1980s, but they did not.

The 1980s did continue some of the trends of the 1970s. The white population continued to age, had fewer children, and slipped into minority status, although it remains the single largest racial group. The subtle revolution of women's entry into the labor force continued and the number of nonfamily households grew. The native-born black and Latino populations continued to increase relative to that of whites and the trends in their female labor force participation rates, birth rates, and household sizes paralleled those of whites. (Labor force participation did not increase among Latino women to the same extent it did among black and white women.)

The differences between the two decades are more striking than the similarities, however. The economic boom of the 1980s and New York City's growing importance as a destination for new immigrants reversed such key trends of the 1970s as population decline, falling real incomes, and the rapid replacement of whites by native-born blacks and Puerto Ricans. Instead, the rapid growth of employment in finance and advanced corporate service industries and public and nonprofit social services slowed the outflow of the white population, attracted new residents, and produced an astounding 26 percent increase in real household income during the decade. (See Appendix Tables 1 and 2.)

Most important, economic growth helped attract new migrants from the Caribbean, Asia, and Latin America. This influx, which began after the reform of immigration laws in 1965, flowered in the 1980s. In the 1990 Census, almost one million of the city's 7.3 million residents said they had arrived from abroad during the last decade. As a result, racial succession took on a new meaning as the foreign-born black and Latino populations grew rapidly. Immigration also increased the city's population relative to that of the suburbs, breaking the pattern of relative decline during the past five decades.

While prosperity and population growth improved many aspects of life in New York City during the 1980s, they also brought new problems. Not everyone benefited from growth; indeed, poverty rates remained high. As a result, overall income inequality increased notably during the decade. In the midst of prosperity in many areas of the city were others who did not share in it and instead experienced deeper and more concentrated misery. As always, racial groups competed for good jobs in the New York City economy and for good homes in its fabric of neighborhoods. Some groups enjoyed advantages over others and the competition among them became more intense.

In contrast to the 1970s, many more neighborhoods improved economically than fell into further decay. Growing proportions of managers and professionals gentrified some of these neighborhoods, both black and white, but more emerged as new immigrant neighborhoods. Several new Chinatowns, a not-so-little Kingston, and little Indias, not to speak of a little Odessa, appeared alongside the old Little Italys. New intergroup tensions and new political cleavages accompanied these trends, but they also set the stage for redefining what it meant to be a New Yorker, a city dweller, and indeed an American.

The severe recession that began at the end of 1989 and bottomed out only in early 1993 further complicated matters. The city lost the jobs it had gained between 1977 and 1989.

Many sectors that had expanded rapidly, such as the investment banking industry, laid off thousands of employees. Unemployment rose to a peak of over 10 percent and poverty increased. With declining revenues, city government was forced to trim the growth of its employment. If the Census had been taken in 1993 instead of 1990, many of the trends portrayed in the following discussion would not be so positive.

As bad as the recession of the early 1990s has been, it was not as devastating as that of the mid-1970s, when the city lost one-sixth of its economic base. New York City government was not forced into near-bankruptcy, and the population does not appear to have fallen in the same way as in the 1970s. The weak real estate market has even enabled many firms to obtain new long-term leases at favorable terms. As the national and world economies recover, New York City will once again be well situated to benefit from their renewed growth.

RACIAL CHANGE

As Chart 1 shows, immigration modified the nature of racial change in New York City during the 1980s. Between 1970 and 1980, the white population plummeted by 1.3 million while the combined black and Latino population grew by 300,000. Between 1980 and 1990, the drop in the white population was cut in half, while the increase in the black and Latino population almost doubled to 572,000. (See Appendix Table 2.) Whites thus became a minority, although they remained the single largest racial group. Immigration accounted for the great majority

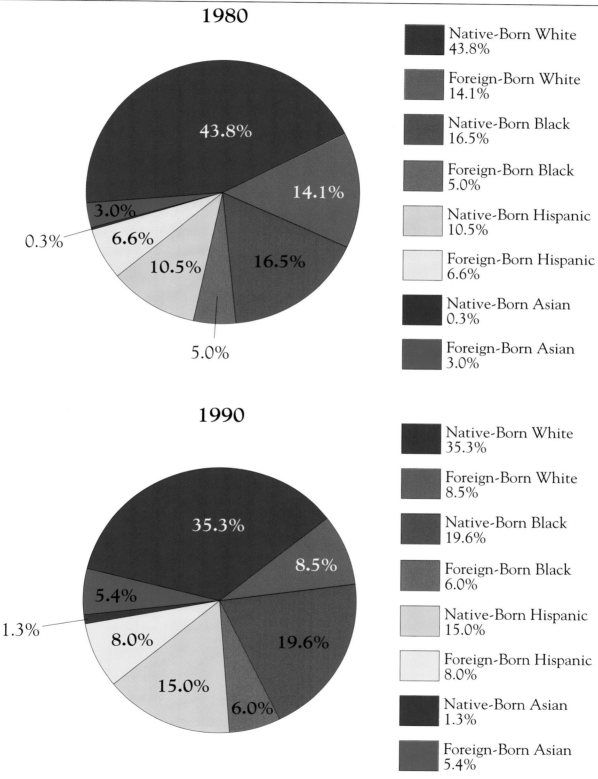

1980

43.8%

14.1%

16.5%

5.0%

10.5%

6.6%

0.3%

3.0%

Native-Born White
43.8%

Foreign-Born White
14.1%

Native-Born Black
16.5%

Foreign-Born Black
5.0%

Native-Born Hispanic
10.5%

Foreign-Born Hispanic
6.6%

Native-Born Asian
0.3%

Foreign-Born Asian
3.0%

1990

35.3%

8.5%

19.6%

6.0%

15.0%

8.0%

1.3%

5.4%

Native-Born White
35.3%

Foreign-Born White
8.5%

Native-Born Black
19.6%

Foreign-Born Black
6.0%

Native-Born Hispanic
15.0%

Foreign-Born Hispanic
8.0%

Native-Born Asian
1.3%

Foreign-Born Asian
5.4%

of population growth among Latinos and a significant portion of the growth among blacks. Table 1 indicates that population declines were greatest among those of English ancestry, followed by the Irish and Italians. Germans and Poles suffered lesser losses, while Greeks dropped the least. By contrast, the population of those of West Indian ancestry grew rapidly, as did the Dominican population.

Map 1, "Residence Patterns of Racial Groups, 1990," shows all the tracts in which whites, blacks, and Latinos make up at least 20 percent of the population and where Asians make up at least 10 percent. These patterns are framed by the high level of racial segregation between blacks (indicated by red cross-hatching) and whites (the tan areas). The few areas where blacks overlap with whites are either where black neighborhoods are expanding into formerly white areas or in a few stable integrated housing developments such as Starrett City in Brooklyn, Co-op City in the Bronx, or the northeastern shore of Staten Island. (In a few instances, such as the Lubavitcher community in Crown Heights or Rochdale Village in Queens, whites have chosen to remain within a larger black neighborhood.) Map 1 also shows that blacks are fairly highly segregated from Asians (horizontal light blue lines). Only on the northern edge of the black community in southeast Queens do the two overlap at all.

Latinos (vertical blue lines) are also segregated from whites, although less so than are blacks, and are segregated from blacks, although less so than are whites. They are more likely to overlap with Asians. The Latino concentrations that have developed in white neighborhoods largely reflect the growth of immigrant communities, such as Jackson Heights, Queens, or Sunset Park, Brooklyn. Latinos and blacks are intermixed only in El Barrio in Manhattan, the South Bronx, and East New York in Brooklyn, and in large public housing projects. Even in these areas, the two may be segregated at a building-by-building or block-by-block level. (Latinos of African descent, who may come from Puerto Rico or the Dominican Republic, live closer to blacks than whites, while Latinos of European or Indian descent live closer to whites and away from blacks.)

TABLE 1
Change in Ethnic Populations, New York City, 1980–1990

Ancestry	1980	1990	Difference
English	306,255	172,709	-43.6
German	453,898	395,230	-12.9
Irish	647,733	535,846	-17.3
Italian	1,005,304	838,878	-16.6
Polish	338,067	296,805	-12.2
Greek	88,920	82,690	-7.0
South American	154,356	219,509	42.2
West Indian	172,192	391,744	127.5
Dominican	124,228	332,713	167.8

Sources: The 1980 Standard Tape File 4 (STF4) and the 1990 STF3, single and multiple ancestry.
Note: Decimal numbers are percentages.

MAP 1
Residence Patterns of Racial Groups, 1990

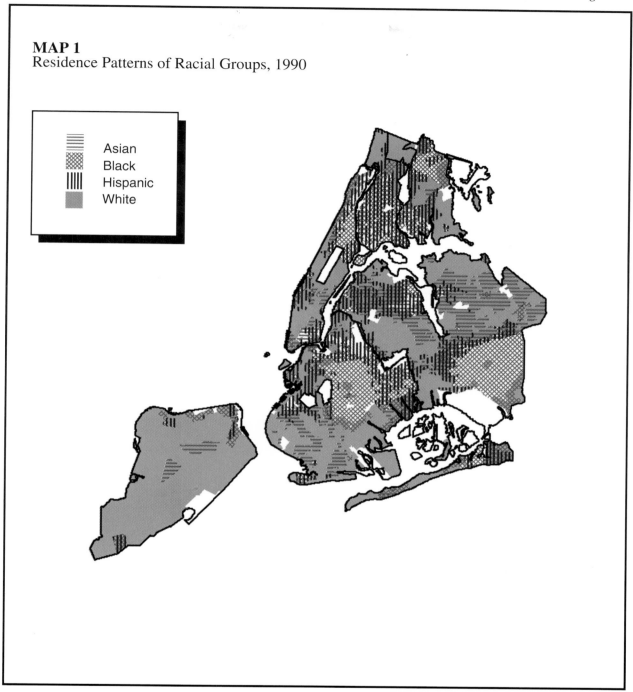

Map 1 shows that Latinos overlap extensively with Asians. The only areas that have many Latinos (mostly Puerto Ricans) and few Asians are in the South Bronx and the West Side of Manhattan. Only in the more suburban parts of eastern Queens and south-western Brooklyn does one find settlements of Asians without Latinos. In short, Latino and Asian groups tend to occupy the spaces between the historic zones of settlement for native-born whites and blacks, with Asians the farthest away from blacks.

Map 2, "Change in White Population, 1980–1990," shows how the white population has shifted over the last decade. Most areas lost white population (the various shades of blue). It grew only in well-established upper middle class areas such as the Upper West Side and Greenwich Village in Manhattan, Park Slope in Brooklyn, and Kew Gardens in Queens; Hasidic neighborhoods such as Borough Park, Crown Heights, and Williamsburg in Queens; and in the areas of Staten Island where new housing is being constructed. White population losses were heaviest in the areas adjacent to growing black and Latino neighborhoods or inside growing immigrant neighborhoods, such as Jackson Heights. In many of these areas, a large percentage of the white residents are more than 65 years old.

Map 3, "Change in Black Population, 1980–1990," shows the shifting pattern of the black population in New York City. The black population declined most strongly in the centers of the old ghettos, which contain the poorest households. It grew most rapidly on the edges of established black neighborhoods, which are also the areas where higher-income West Indian blacks are most likely to live. Map 4, "Change in Latino Population, 1980–1990," shows that the Latino population has declined (or grown most slowly) in areas of black settlement, and expanded most in existing barrios (East Harlem, Williamsburg-Bushwick, the South Bronx) and in areas of new immigrant settlement (Sunset Park, Jackson Heights). Map 5, "Change in Asian Population, 1980–1990," shows a similar pattern for the movement of the Asian population, which declined in areas where

blacks and Puerto Ricans are concentrated and grew most rapidly in Chinatown, Elmhurst, Flushing, Sunset Park, and the Bloomfield area of Staten Island, where new housing is under construction.

Maps 6–9 show how predominantly white, black, Latino, and Asian areas differ by income.[2] These patterns strongly resemble differences in levels of education, which are not shown. These maps show that New Yorkers are strongly segregated by income as well as by race. Map 6, "Median White Household Income, White Tracts, 1990," shows that the wealthiest whites live in the Upper East and West Sides of Manhattan and in outer borough neighborhoods such as Moshulu in the Bronx; Kew Gardens and Little Neck in Queens; Brooklyn Heights, Park Slope, and Bay Ridge in Brooklyn; and Todt Hill in Staten Island. Aging white ethnic neighborhoods have the lowest incomes for white households, and they are often adjacent to expanding minority neighborhoods.

Map 7, "Median Black Household Income, Black Tracts, 1990," shows that, while blacks are on average much less well off than whites, they are also spatially separated according to income. A few black enclaves have median incomes similar to those in the highest category of the white population: University Heights and Eastchester in the Bronx and sections of Flushing, Jamaica, Hollis, and especially Laurelton and

---

[2]The white, black, and Asian median household categories include Latinos who told the Census they were one of these races. Just under half of all Latinos said they were white, about 40 percent said "other," and about 15 percent said black.

MAP 2
Change in White Population, 1980–1990

Number

-6,729 to -764
-763 to -351
-350 to 0
1 to 99
100 to 5,374

MAP 3
Change in Black Population, 1980–1990

Number

-1,371 to -30
-29 to 0
1 to 99
100 to 399
400 to 4,993

MAP 4
Change in Latino Population, 1980–1990

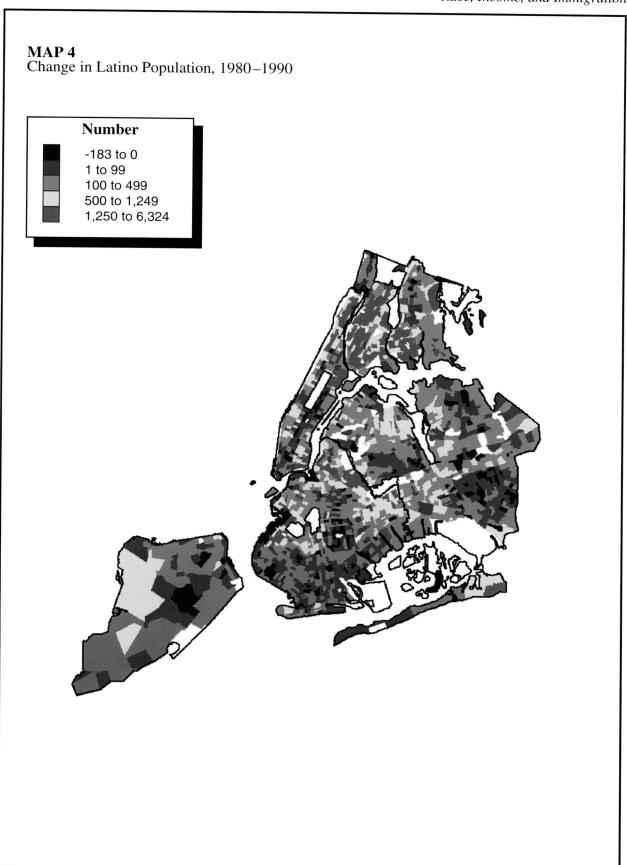

Number
- -183 to 0
- 1 to 99
- 100 to 499
- 500 to 1,249
- 1,250 to 6,324

MAP 5
Change in Asian Population, 1980–1990

Number

-370 to 0
1 to 49
50 to 299
300 to 499
500 to 3,283

MAP 6
Median White Household Income, White Tracts, 1990

Dollars

- 0 to 21,999
- 22,000 to 44,999
- 45,000 to 59,999
- 60,000 to 69,999
- 70,000 to 262,026

MAP 7
Median Black Household Income, Black Tracts, 1990

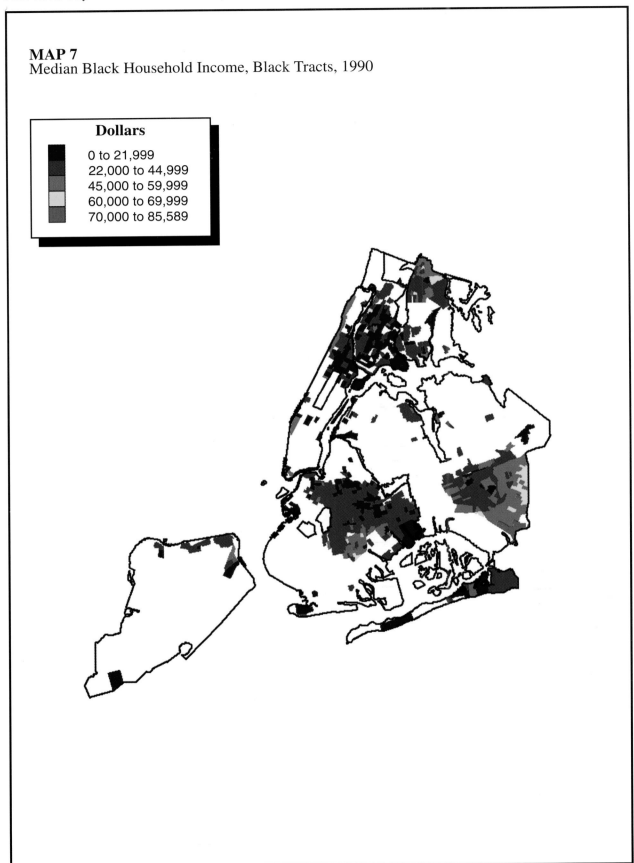

Dollars

0 to 21,999
22,000 to 44,999
45,000 to 59,999
60,000 to 69,999
70,000 to 85,589

MAP 8
Median Latino Household Income, Latino Tracts, 1990

Dollars

0 to 21,999
22,000 to 44,999
45,000 to 59,999
60,000 to 69,999
70,000 to 299,053

MAP 9
Median Asian Household Income, Asian Tracts, 1990

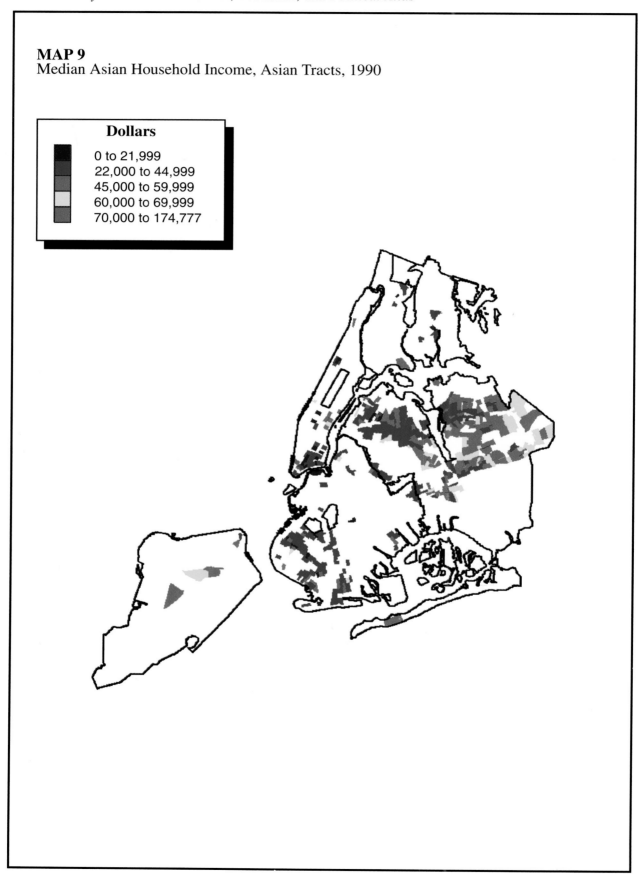

Dollars

0 to 21,999
22,000 to 44,999
45,000 to 59,999
60,000 to 69,999
70,000 to 174,777

Rosedale in Queens. Blacks living on the south side of the Caribbean enclave in Flatbush and the east side of the Caribbean enclave of southeast Queens also have relatively high incomes. Blacks with the lowest incomes live in the old ghetto cores in Harlem, Bedford-Stuyvesant, and the South Bronx.

Map 8, "Median Latino Household Income, Latino Tracts, 1990," shows that Latinos are even less well off than blacks, although there are a few tiny enclaves of well-off Latinos. As with blacks, well-off Latinos live on the peripheries of expanding immigrant settlements such as Jackson Heights, while the poorest Latinos live in the Puerto Rican barrios of East Harlem, the South Bronx, and Williamsburg-Bushwick in Brooklyn. Finally, Map 9, "Median Asian Household Income, Asian Tracts, 1990," shows that Asian households tend to have higher incomes than do blacks or Latinos. The highest income Asian households live in suburban eastern Queens, while the poorest are in Chinatown. The heavily immigrant areas of Elmhurst, Flushing, and Sunset Park neither fall in the higher-income categories, nor do they fall in the lowest category where so many black and Latino tracts are found.

IMMIGRATION AND ETHNICITY

In the last century, successive waves of Irish, German, Italian, and Jewish immigrants made an imprint on New York City and on other large American cities that is still visible three generations later. Their struggle to become part of the economic, cultural, and political fabric redefined the nature of city life and what it meant to be American. In 1890, 39 percent of New York and Brooklyn's combined population of 2.3 million were foreign born. By 1930, the newly consolidated city's population had risen to 6.9 million, of whom 34 percent were foreign born.

New immigrants are once more transforming the city's population, neighborhoods, and social fabric. Since the reform of national immigration laws in 1965, an annual average of about 80,000 migrants from the Caribbean, Latin America, and Asia have settled in New York. One-fourth of all immigrants to the United States currently enter through New York City, and one-sixth have chosen to reside there; only Los Angeles has attracted more. Together, the two metropolitan areas have attracted 40 percent of all migrants to the United States.

Just as they did a century ago, these immigrants have moved to New York because it offers opportunities they cannot find at home. More than virtually any other city, New York is open to newcomers and willing to be shaped by them. As a result, as E. B. White wrote forty-five years ago, "The collision and the intermingling of these millions of foreign-born people representing so many races and creeds make New York a permanent exhibit of the phenomenon of one world" (*Here Is New York*, E. B. White [New York: Harper and Brothers, 1949] 42–3).

In 1990, almost one million of the people who lived in New York City told the Census that they had arrived from abroad since 1980. Besides reversing the decades-long decrease of the city's population, these new New Yorkers have strongly reshaped the city's neighborhoods, cultural fabric, and economy. According to the 1990 Census, 28.4 percent of the city's population was foreign born. If Puerto Ricans were included in this count (although they are U.S. citizens, they emigrated from a Spanish-speaking Caribbean island culture), today's immigrant percentage would approach the figure reached at the turn of the century. If the count included undocumented immigrants, it might even exceed that figure.

Between 1982 and 1989, the Immigration and Naturalization Service granted permanent residence status to almost 700,000 people who declared that they were going to reside in the city. For more information see *The Newest New Yorkers: An Analysis of Immigration into New York City During the 1980s,* Joseph J. Salvo et al. (New York: New York City Department of City Planning, 1992). The top ten sending countries were the Dominican Republic (116,000), Jamaica (72,000), the People's Republic of China (72,000), Guyana (54,000), Haiti (41,000), Colombia (23,000), India (20,000), Korea (20,000), Ecuador (18,000), and the Philippines (14,000). Grouped by region, about one-third came from the Spanish-speaking Caribbean and Central and South America, about one-quarter from the rest of the Caribbean, and another quarter from Asia. (The rest came mainly from Europe; Africa contributed only 2 percent of the total.)

These new immigrants have different racial and national backgrounds than those of a century ago, but they are just as vital to the city today as the old white Catholic and Jewish immigrants were to the garment and construction industries, the needle trades and construction unions, and city politics. Without today's Afro-Caribbean, Latino, and Asian immigrants, many manufacturing industries would have declined even more than they have. The new immigrants are also crucial to the growth of service industries like hotels and health care institutions. Immigrant enterprises, serving both ethnic enclaves and broader markets, have diversified consumer choice in restaurants, fruit and vegetable markets, and many other retail activities. New York is one of the few places where one can take a trip around the world within the city limits.

Map 10, "Foreign Born, 1990," shows where the highest percentages of native-born (red) and foreign-born (blue) populations live in New York City. Both black and white neighborhoods show the largest concentrations of the native born. In Manhattan, they are found in Harlem and the Village; in Brooklyn, Bedford-Stuyvesant and Dyker Heights; in Queens, South Jamaica and Bayside. It is worth noting, however, that almost every part of New York City contains at least some immigrants. The highest concentrations of immigrants are in Washington Heights, Chinatown, Astoria, Elmhurst, Jackson Heights, Flushing, Flatbush, and Brighton Beach.

Because Europeans represent such a small proportion of the total, recent white immigrants predominate in only a few neighborhoods, most notably the Russian Jewish settlement in Brighton Beach, Brooklyn, and the Polish enclave of Greenpoint. The imprint of the last century's European migration may be seen in Maps 11–14, which show where their descendants now reside. They are no longer in the original zones of settlement, such as the Lower East Side. Instead, they live either in the long-established middle and upper middle class neighborhoods of

MAP 10
Foreign Born, 1990

Percent

- 0 to 9
- 10 to 17
- 18 to 27
- 28 to 39
- 40 to 82

MAP 11
Jewish Ancestries Population, 1990

Number

0
1 to 99
100 to 649
650 to 1,999
2,000 to 4,351

MAP 12
Italian Ancestry Population, 1990

Number

0
1 to 99
100 to 499
500 to 1,999
2,000 to 9,200

MAP 13
Irish Ancestry Population, 1990

Number

0
1 to 49
50 to 449
450 to 1,499
1,500 to 3,300

MAP 14
German Ancestry Population, 1990

Number

0
1 to 49
50 to 329
330 to 999
1,000 to 1,860

Manhattan, such as the Upper East Side and the Upper West Side, or on the suburban coastal peripheries of the rest of the city.

The two largest groups in the early twentieth century migration to New York were Italians and Jews leaving Russia, Poland, and Hungary. These three latter ancestries generally represent those of Jewish heritage. Today, as shown by Map 11, "Jewish Ancestries Population, 1990," those who told the Census they were from these ancestries are concentrated on the East Side and West Side of Manhattan and in Stuyvesant Town. Only a few areas of Manhattan remain predominantly Italian American, however, as Map 12, "Italian Ancestry Population, 1990," shows.

Outside Manhattan, people of Jewish or Italian heritage tend to dominate the suburban neighborhoods on the periphery of the city. These groups overlap in some areas, such as Bergen Beach, Canarsie, and Howard Beach, but they usually exist in distinct clusters. The biggest Italian-American concentrations to be seen in Map 12 are on Staten Island; in Brooklyn's Dyker Heights, Bensonhurst, and Gravesend neighborhoods; Howard Beach in Queens; and Schuylerville in the Bronx. Map 11 shows that the biggest concentrations of Jewish ancestries outside Manhattan are in Borough Park, Midwood, Gravesend, Sheepshead Bay, Mill Basin, and Canarsie in Brooklyn, and the band of neighborhoods running from Rego Park, Forest Hills, and Kew Gardens through the garden apartment complexes of Windsor Park Apartments, Bell Park Gardens, and Oakland Gardens, to Glen Oaks in Queens. Bayside is another area of Jewish concentration. The largest Jewish neighborhoods remaining in the Bronx are

Riverdale and Co-op City. Of these neighborhoods, Jewish immigrants from the former Soviet Union have had the largest impact on Brighton Beach.

The two biggest groups of the mid-nineteenth century immigration, the Germans and the Irish, have a stronger tendency to reside near each other than do those of Jewish and Italian ancestries and do not overlap greatly with either of these groups. (The descendants of German Jewish immigrants have a different settlement pattern than those descended from Protestant or Catholic German immigrants.) In Manhattan, those of German and Irish descent live in the middle to upper middle class neighborhoods of the East and West Sides, Stuyvesant Town, and the Village. The Irish have joined Italian Americans in making Staten Island a predominantly white ethnic, Catholic borough. Although Germans were once the largest group in Brooklyn, few of their descendants remain. Irish enclaves remain in Windsor Terrace and Bay Ridge.

Queens and the Bronx have more Irish-German neighborhoods. Cut off from the rest of the city by cemeteries and railroad lines, the Queens neighborhoods of Woodside, Middle Village, Ridgewood, and Glendale retain the flavor of the working or lower middle class Irish-German neighborhoods that characterized the city a century ago. The largest concentrations of Irish Americans outside Manhattan can be found, according to Map 13, "Irish Ancestry Population, 1990," in Norwood in the Bronx, Gerretsen Beach in Brooklyn, Breezy Point and Rockaway Park in Queens, and Arden Heights and Annadale in Staten Island. Irish immigrants may be found in Woodside and Norwood. Map 14, "German Ancestry Population, 1990," shows that, aside from Stuyvesant Town, Yorkville, the West Side, and Overlook Terrace in Inwood (a German Jewish settlement), the highest German-American concentrations are in Glendale and Middle Village in Queens near the Lutheran cemetery and in Arden Heights in Staten Island.

Recent immigrants have had a pervasive impact on black and Latino neighborhoods. Afro-Caribbean concentrations are centered in Flatbush in Brooklyn, Jamaica and Hollis in Queens, and Williamsbridge in the Bronx. Map 15, "West Indian and Black Population, 1990," shows that West Indian immigrants have not settled in the large, long-standing African-American neighborhoods of Harlem or Bedford-Stuyvesant. Instead, they have settled on the expanding peripheries of black settlement areas outside of Manhattan, particularly in Flatbush in Brooklyn, southeast Queens, and the north central Bronx. Map 16, "West Indian Ancestry Population, 1990," shows that the single biggest West Indian concentration is on the western and eastern edges of Flatbush and that the West Indian areas of Williamsbridge and Wakefield, north of Seton Falls Park in the Bronx, are the second biggest. Because the expanding West Indian neighborhoods of southeast Queens have a low population density, they do not show up as a large concentration, but they too are an important area of settlement. These West Indian neighborhoods are the areas where the black population as a whole is expanding into older white ethnic areas with declining white populations. This has put a Caribbean face on the pattern of racial

succession in New York City.

Map 17, "Latino Immigrant and Puerto Rican Population, 1990," shows where the Dominican and South American immigrants have settled in relation to established Puerto Rican neighborhoods. As with blacks, it shows that Latino immigrants have mainly not settled in the long-established Puerto Rican neighborhoods, but instead have developed their own areas at some distance from them. The largest Puerto Rican settlements are in the South Bronx; El Barrio (East Harlem) and the Lower East Side in Manhattan; and Williamsburg, Bushwick, and Sunset Park in Brooklyn, as Map 18 "Puerto Rican Population, 1990," shows. The largest Latino immigrant group, Dominicans, did not settle in the Puerto Rican neighborhoods of El Barrio or the South Bronx. Instead, Map 19, "Dominican Population, 1990," shows they are heavily concentrated east of Broadway in Washington Heights and Inwood in northern Manhattan.

Another important Dominican settlement exists across the Harlem River in the western parts of the South Bronx. Here, in Morris Heights and Tremont, Dominicans are intermingled with Puerto Ricans. Although Dominicans may also be found in the predominantly Puerto Rican areas of the Lower East Side, Williamsburg, and the part of Bushwick adjacent to Most Holy Trinity Cemetery, the next largest settlement of Dominicans after Washington Heights is in the South American zone in Jackson Heights and Corona in Queens.

The largest concentration of South Americans is found far from either the predominantly Puerto Rican or the predominantly Dominican parts of the city. Map 20, "South

MAP 15
West Indian and Black Population, 1990

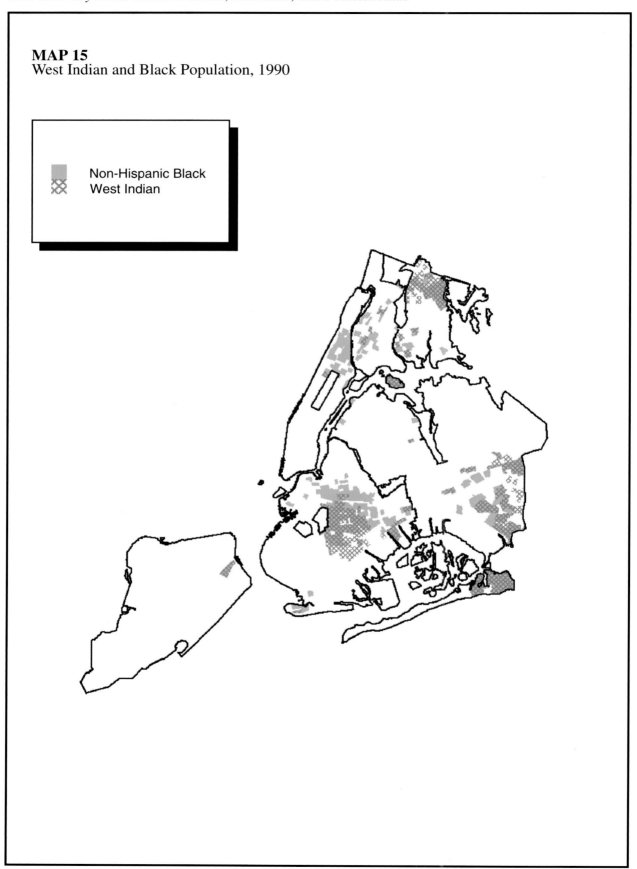

Non-Hispanic Black
West Indian

MAP 16
West Indian Ancestry Population, 1990

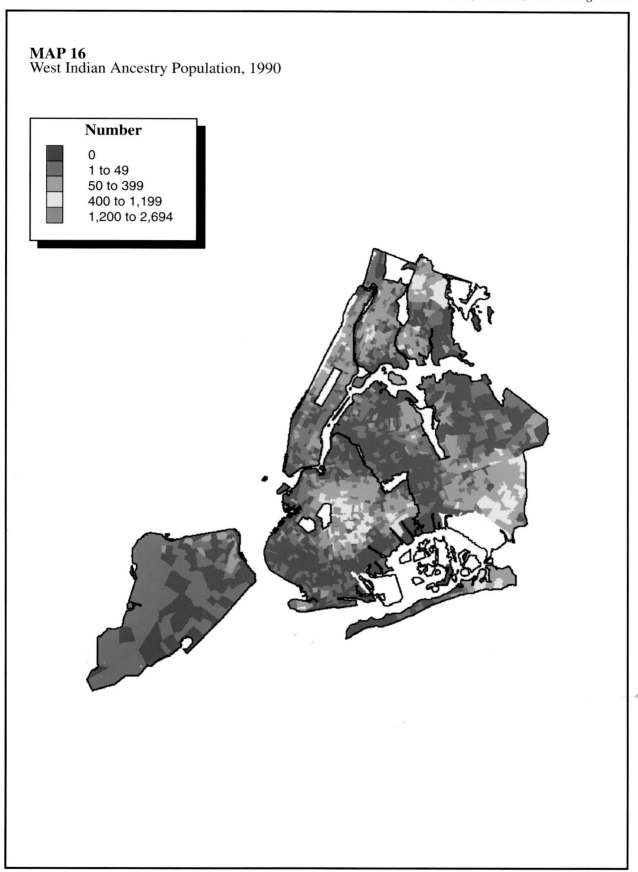

Number

0
1 to 49
50 to 399
400 to 1,199
1,200 to 2,694

MAP 17
Latino Immigrant and Puerto Rican Population, 1990

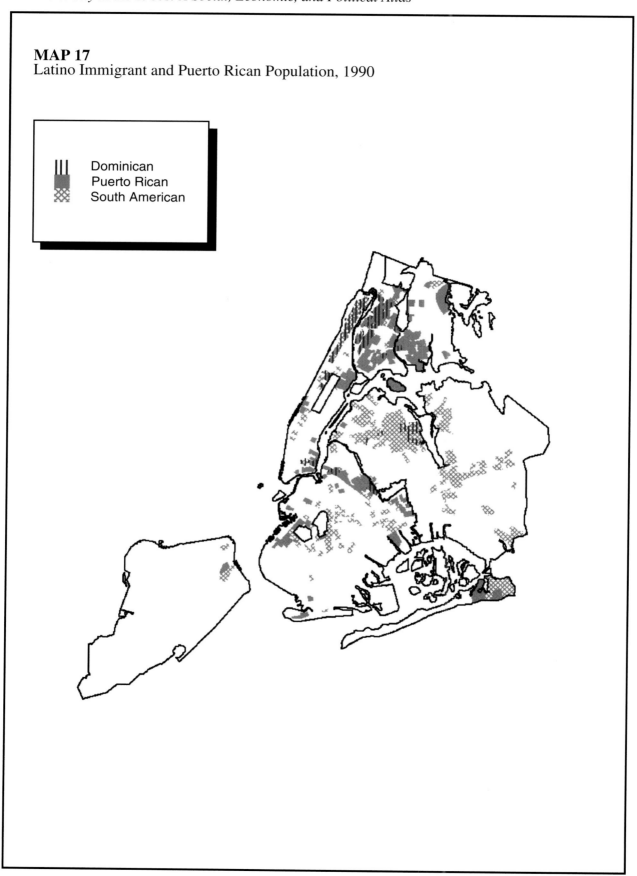

Dominican
Puerto Rican
South American

MAP 18
Puerto Rican Population, 1990

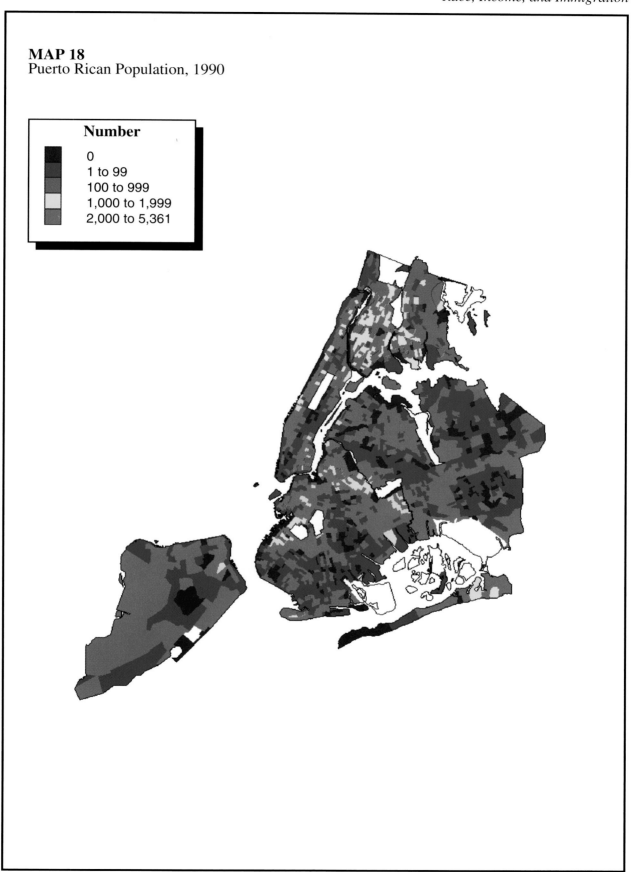

MAP 19
Dominican Population, 1990

Number

0
1 to 99
100 to 999
1,000 to 1,999
2,000 to 8,547

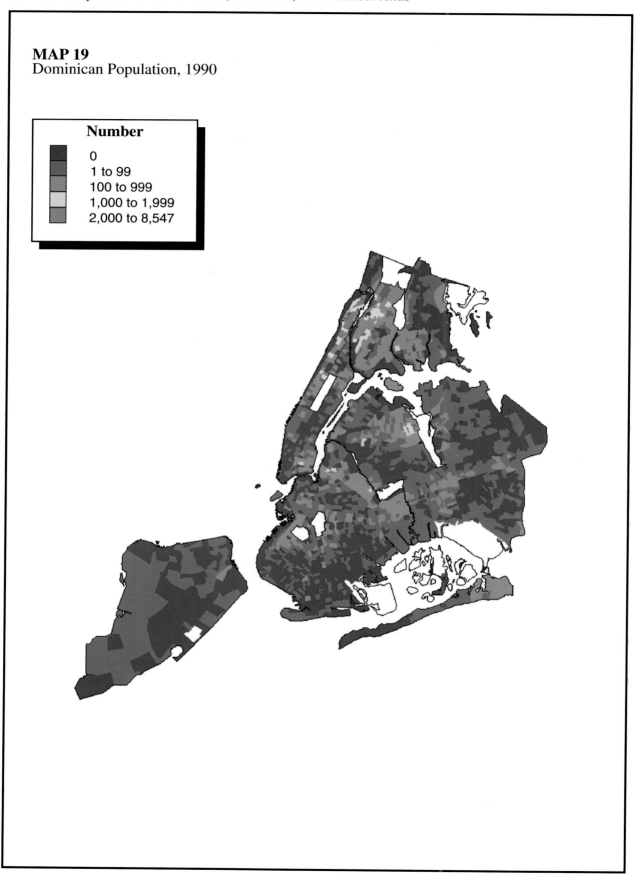

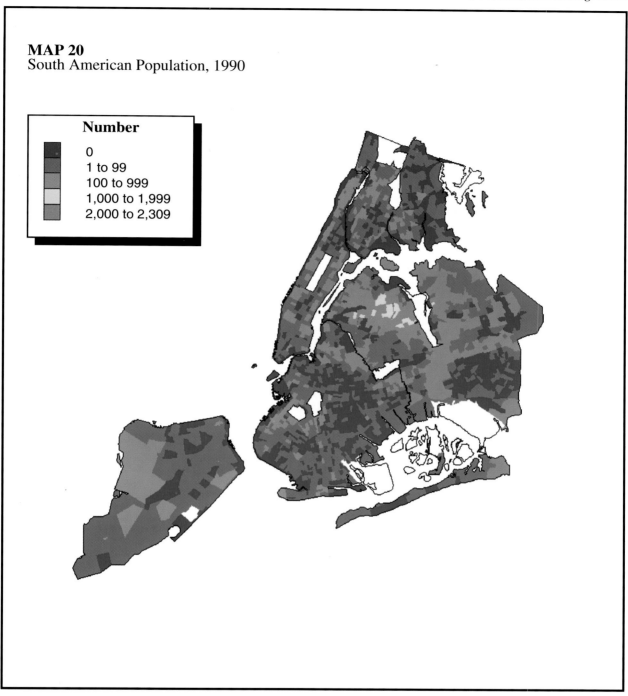

MAP 20
South American Population, 1990

Number
0
1 to 99
100 to 999
1,000 to 1,999
2,000 to 2,309

American Population, 1990," shows that, although there are far fewer South Americans than Puerto Ricans or Dominicans in New York City, large numbers live along Roosevelt Avenue in Jackson Heights, in Corona, and adjacent to New Calvary Cemetery in Sunny-side. In lower numbers and concentrations, they are spread across Queens and in other Latino areas of New York City, particularly Sunset Park and Washington Heights.

Map 21, "Asian Populations, 1990," confirms that Asians have settled away from

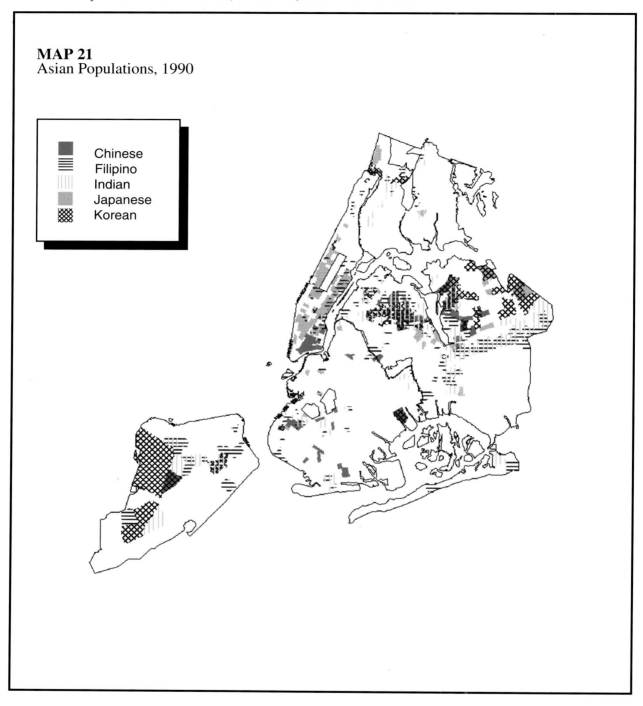

MAP 21
Asian Populations, 1990

Chinese
Filipino
Indian
Japanese
Korean

African Americans and Puerto Ricans, but closer to Latino immigrant groups. Like the white ethnic groups, Asian groups have combined in several different ways. Map 22, "Chinese Population, 1990," shows that the largest Asian group, the Chinese, have estab- lished major concentrations not only in Manhattan's Chinatown, but in the new Chinatowns of Elmhurst and Flushing, Queens, and Sunset Park, Brooklyn. While other Asian groups have not been attracted to Chinatown in great numbers, Indians,

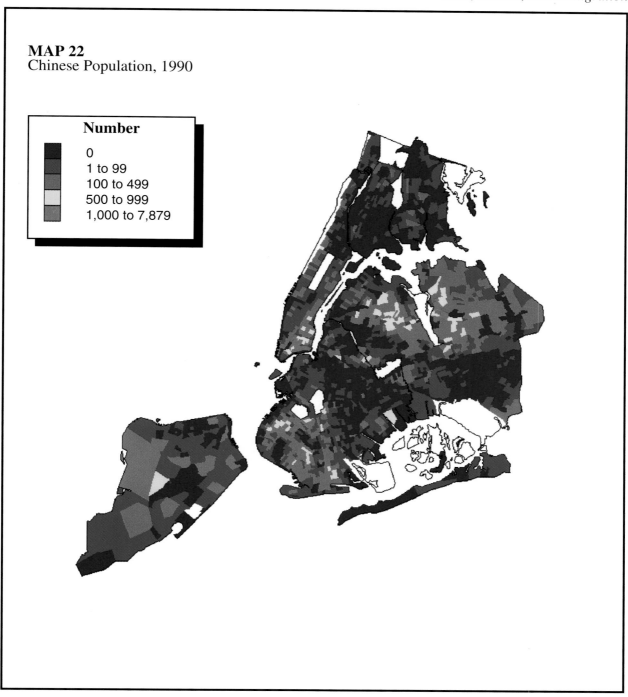

MAP 22
Chinese Population, 1990

Number
- 0
- 1 to 99
- 100 to 499
- 500 to 999
- 1,000 to 7,879

Filipinos, and Koreans have settled around the Chinese concentrations in Elmhurst and Flushing. Indians and Filipinos have also created their own settlement area between the black and white areas of eastern Queens. (The Japanese, it should be noted, have a quite distinct settlement pattern, more likely to follow that of upper middle class whites.)

As two of the highest-income immigrant groups, Indians and Filipinos are also found adjacent to each other in the Jewish neighborhoods north of Jamaica Avenue in eastern

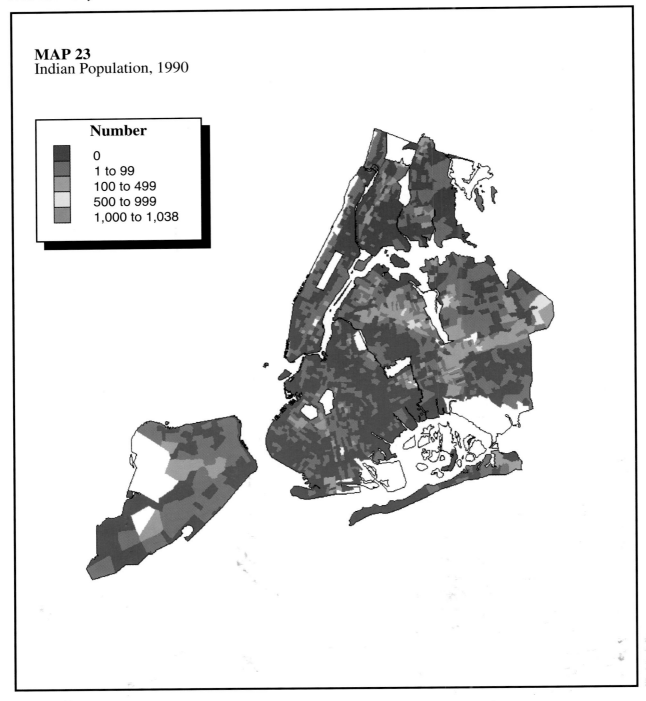

MAP 23
Indian Population, 1990

Number
- 0
- 1 to 99
- 100 to 499
- 500 to 999
- 1,000 to 1,038

Queens, as Map 23, "Indian Population, 1990," shows for the Indians. One interesting departure from this pattern is the Indian concentration south of Liberty Avenue in South Jamaica, where Guyanese and Trinidadians of East Indian ancestry are also found.

Map 24, "Korean Population, 1990," shows that Koreans have settled not only in the Asian concentrations of Elmhurst and Flushing, but also in other middle class parts of northeastern Queens and some of the developing parts of Staten Island.

MAP 24
Korean Population, 1990

Number

- 0
- 1 to 99
- 100 to 499
- 500 to 999
- 1,000 to 2,193

Section II

Social Problems and Community Resources

The demographic and economic shifts of the 1980s had a profound but uneven impact on New York City neighborhoods and residents. The economic boom meant more New Yorkers held jobs, that the average New Yorker had a rising real household income, and that the housing stock improved in most neighborhoods. The proportion of white families even increased in some areas that had become more black in the previous decade.

This prosperity was unevenly distributed, however. Whites gained most, blacks held their own, and Latinos slipped downward relative to the other two groups. Among blacks and Latinos, immigrants on the whole tended to do better than the native born, although many African Americans and Puerto Ricans were upwardly mobile during this period. Although the decennial Censuses indicated that the poverty rate fell slightly between 1980 and 1990, it remained stubbornly high and increased in some areas. The Census Bureau also measures poverty annually through its Current Population Survey, which suggests that New York City's poverty rate may be higher than the 1990 Census indicated and was rising in the early 1990s with the onset of the recession. Finally, during the 1980s, income inequality widened among whites, blacks, and Latinos and such new problems as AIDS, the crack epidemic, and homelessness emerged. Intergroup tensions also took on new forms.

The pattern of changing employment given in Map 25, "Change in Employed Persons, 1980–1990," shows where the active labor force grew in the city. This number increased when more people living in these neighborhoods got jobs or when people who already held jobs moved into the neighborhoods or both. Some of the largest gains occurred in areas one might expect: Battery Park City, the Upper East Side, and the Upper West Side, and the newly developed area of Staten Island. But immigrant neighborhoods also showed strong gains, especially the Haitian community on the west edge of Caribbean Flatbush; the Asian concentrations in Chinatown, Elmhurst, and Flushing; and Dominican northern Manhattan. Most areas that lost or gained the fewest employed residents were in or near the declining industrial areas of the outer boroughs, such as on either side of Newtown Creek in Greenpoint and Hunters Point and Woodside. The fewest job gains also were registered in the centers of the Puerto Rican and native-born black population over this period.

The changing pattern of income distribution is starkly illustrated in Map 26, "Change in Median Household Income, 1980–1990." The red and yellow areas show the highest income gains, and they occurred mostly in upper middle class white neighborhoods, which include the Upper East Side, Tribeca, Battery Park City in Manhattan; Brooklyn Heights, Park Slope, Flatlands, and Mill Basin in Brooklyn; the middle class white areas of Queens; much of Staten Island; and Riverdale in the Bronx.

The areas with declining incomes or the lowest income gains were firmly centered in areas long settled by African Americans and Puerto Ricans, including Harlem, El Barrio, the South Bronx, Williamsburg, Bushwick, and Bedford-Stuyvesant. (Blacks and Puerto Ricans who did well between 1980 and 1990 may have left New York City.) A few white

MAP 25
Change in Employed Persons, 1980–1990

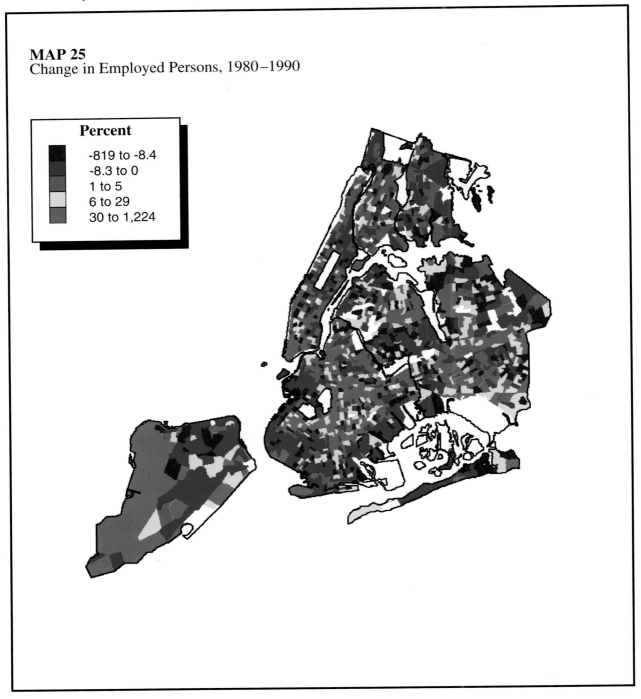

Percent

■	-819 to -8.4
■	-8.3 to 0
■	1 to 5
□	6 to 29
■	30 to 1,224

ethnic areas, such as Bensonhurst, also did not perform well. Areas with large Dominican and Asian populations also made only modest gains. But areas where the West Indian population was expanding experienced substantial income gains, suggesting that West Indians not only improved their position over the decade but had higher incomes than the white families they were replacing in these areas.

Changing patterns of income inequality are demonstrated even more starkly in Map

MAP 26
Change in Median Household Income, 1980–1990

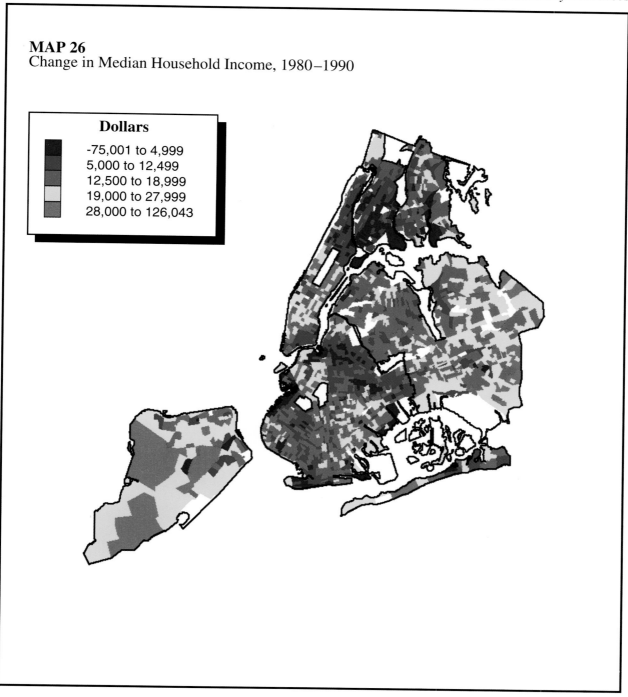

Dollars

-75,001 to 4,999
5,000 to 12,499
12,500 to 18,999
19,000 to 27,999
28,000 to 126,043

27, "Change in Income from Dividends, Interest, and Rent, 1980–1990," which shows changes in unearned income from wealth for households receiving such income. Because much of the boom of the 1980s took the form of returns to financial assets rather than wages and salaries, this map clearly shows that the benefits of the boom of the 1980s were concentrated in upper middle class white areas, while losses or the least gains were concentrated in black and Latino areas. Map 28, "Poverty Rate, 1990," shows that the

MAP 27
Change in Income from Dividends, Interest, and Rent, 1980–1990

Percent

-22 to 4
5 to 12
13 to 25
26 to 34
35 to 100

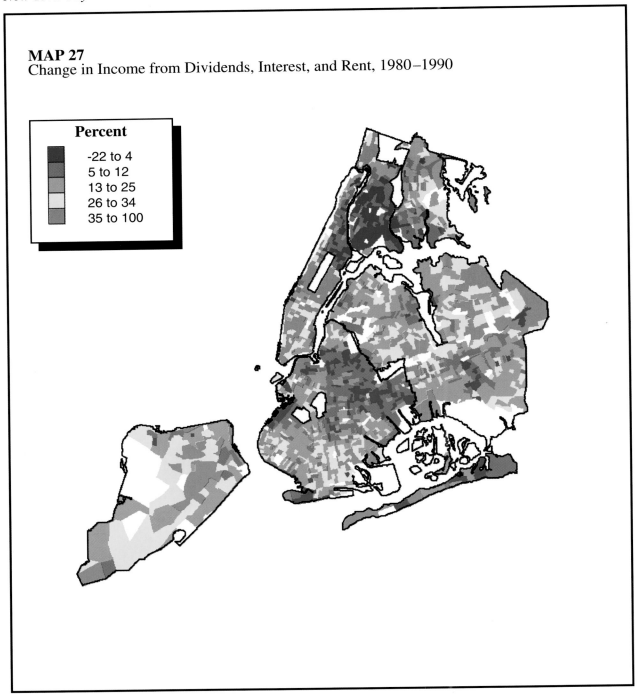

highest poverty rates were concentrated in Puerto Rican and, to a lesser extent, African-American neighborhoods.

Two of the main factors that contribute to poverty are low labor force participation rates for men and women and the rising number of female-headed households, many of which rely on Aid to Families with Dependent Children (AFDC). Map 29, "Adult Men Not in the Labor Force, 1990," shows the percentage of working-age men who are not in the labor force. Areas (in red) with the lowest rates of

MAP 28
Poverty Rate, 1990

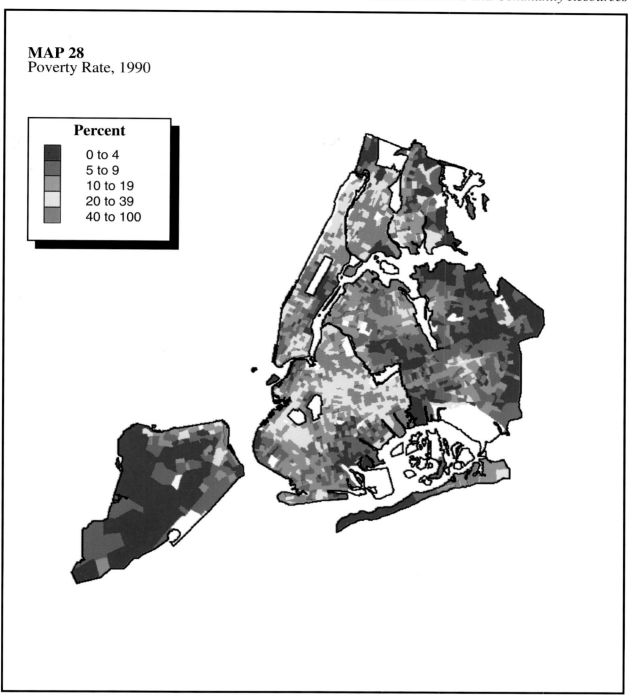

Percent

	0 to 4
	5 to 9
	10 to 19
	20 to 39
	40 to 100

men working (the highest rates of nonpartici-pation) tend to be tracts containing hospitals, public housing projects, or thinly populated declining industrial areas. High rates of nonparticipation are found primarily in the ghettos and barrios, although some tracts within these areas do better than others.

Immigrant blacks and Latinos, have higher labor force participation rates than native-born blacks and Puerto Ricans, as can be seen in the contrasts between Dominican Washington Heights and Puerto Rican areas

MAP 29
Adult Men Not in the Labor Force, 1990

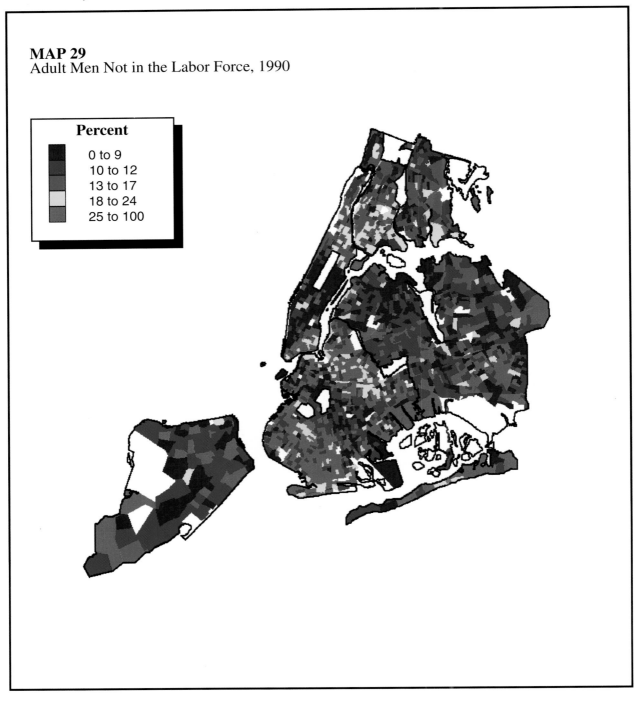

Percent

0 to 9
10 to 12
13 to 17
18 to 24
25 to 100

of the South Bronx or between African-American Bedford-Stuyvesant and West Indian Flatbush. Indeed, immigrant black and Latino men appear to have higher rates of labor force participation than do men in many of the aging white ethnic neighborhoods of the outer boroughs. Areas of Hasidic Jewish settlement in particular seem to have lower labor force participation rates than other white ethnic neighborhoods.

These patterns are presented even more clearly in Map 30, "Adult Women Not in

MAP 30
Adult Women Not in the Labor Force, 1990

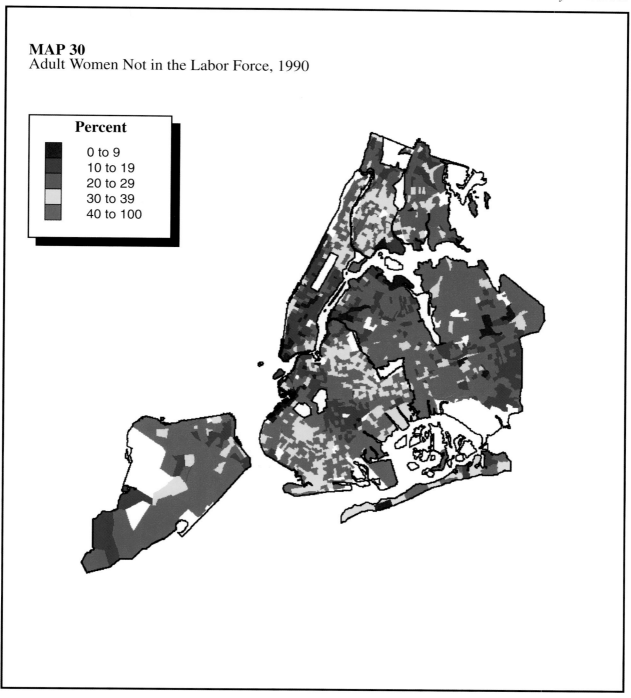

Percent

0 to 9
10 to 19
20 to 29
30 to 39
40 to 100

the Labor Force, 1990," which shows the percentage of adult women not participating in the labor force. The highest rates of nonparticipation (red and yellow) are found in predominantly Puerto Rican areas, followed by African-American areas. Tracts with housing projects have particularly high rates of nonparticipation. West Indian women, however, have rates of participation that are higher not only than in native-born black or Puerto Rican areas, but higher than in either Latin or Asian immigrant areas or in the Irish,

Italian, and Jewish neighborhoods of southern Brooklyn. The highest rates of female labor force participation are found, however, in white neighborhoods with many professionals, such as the Upper East or West Sides or Park Slope in Brooklyn.

Because most families in New York City must rely on more than one income, it is especially important to consider the overlap between the patterns for men and women. Poverty is especially prevalent where large percentages of men and women are out of the labor force. Even though West Indians tend to have jobs in the lower half of the wage spectrum, the fact that both men and women typically have jobs puts their families higher on the income scale and makes them better off than most other immigrant or minority groups. Similarly, the fact that many women as well as many men in the upper middle class professional neighborhoods have jobs raises their household incomes to the top of the distribution.

The industry of one's employment and one's occupation also explains much about one's income. Appendix Tables 3 and 4 show how employed members of the different groups are distributed across different industries and occupations. They show that, among white ethnic groups, those of English, German, and Jewish ancestries are most likely to work in finance, insurance, real estate, corporate services, education, and social services sectors of the economy. Most are managers or professionals. Those of Italian ancestry are more likely to be in the construction, transportation, and retail industries and administrative, crafts, and machine operative occupations.

Native-born blacks are more likely to work in the personal services, health services, education, other social services, and government. Compared with whites, not many native-born blacks are managers or professionals; they are more likely to be clerical or service workers. Immigrant blacks are found in the same general sectors as native-born blacks and in construction and transportation, although they are more likely to be managers and professionals.

The Puerto Rican population also has a low rate of managers and professionals, although it was slightly higher than for blacks. Puerto Ricans, too, are concentrated in the low wage service sectors, with low percentages in finance or corporate services. Puerto Ricans work in retail, personal services, and health services, while immigrant Latinos are more concentrated in durable manufacturing, the garment industry, and wholesale; they are even lower in the occupational order. Puerto Ricans, however, have the lowest rate of participation in the labor force of any group. Among Latino immigrants, South Americans have the highest rate of self-employment. Finally, Asian immigrants are found in the restaurant and apparel industries, although the Indians are also in finance and corporate services. Asians, too, tend to be service workers and operate machines.

The income trajectories of these groups depend on whether they are in the labor force and on what is happening to the industries and occupations in which they work. Those who held high-level jobs in growing sectors, such as people of English or Jewish ancestries, benefited most during the 1980s. Those who held lower-level jobs in industries that did well but not spectacularly, such as the African Americans who work in government and social services, held their own. Those who had blue collar jobs in declining industries, such as Latinos working in the garment industry, fared least well over the decade. Of course, those who did not work fared worst of all because the value of welfare benefits in real dollars declined precipitously.

The consequences of these trends may be seen in various health indicators, which are available at the zip code level. One important consequence of poverty and lack of access to medical services is infant mortality. Map 31, "Infant Deaths Per 1,000 Live Births, 1990," shows that the highest mortality rates are found in Harlem, Bushwick, Bedford-Stuyvesant, Sunset Park, East New York, and South Jamaica. Another indicator strongly linked to poverty is the percentage of babies born at lower than normal birth weight, shown in Map 32, "Low Birth Weight Relative to Live Births, 1990." It, too, shows Harlem and Jamaica, Queens, to have the worst problem, along with the South Bronx, Bushwick, Bedford-Stuyvesant, Coney Island, and other parts of southeast Queens also represented. Again, this problem is not as severe in Asian, Dominican, or West Indian areas, except for the West Indian area of the north central Bronx.

Map 33, "AIDS Deaths in 1990," shows deaths caused by AIDS and AIDS-related diseases. While these deaths were high in areas where gay men live, such as the Upper West Side and the West Village, they were also high in poor Latino and black areas such as Harlem, East Harlem, the South Bronx, Bushwick, Bedford-Stuyvesant, and East

New York. One reason that AIDS has become so prevalent in these areas has to do with drug use. The close spatial relation between AIDS and drug use can be seen in Map 34, "Drug Deaths in 1990," which shows that drug-related deaths are also numerous in poor Puerto Rican and African-American areas such as El Barrio, the South Bronx, East New York, and Bedford-Stuyvesant. Black and Latino immigrant neighborhoods have fewer drug-related deaths, as do most white areas except for the Upper West Side and Riverdale. Suicide, however, is much less associated with poverty, as Map 35, "Suicides in 1990," shows. The highest number of suicides is found in the upper middle class white areas of the Upper East Side and Upper West Side.

The incidence of killings shown in Map 36, "Homicides in 1990," closely parallels that of drug deaths, but Washington Heights, the South Bronx, and central Brooklyn stand out even more starkly. (There were 56 people killed in zip code 10453 in the Bronx.) More homicides occurred in Bedford-Stuyvesant than in Harlem; the number was also high in the Haitian part of the West Indian enclave in Flatbush.

New York has an extensive network of social service agencies designed to combat such ills as AIDS and drug use. Map 37, "Social Service Organizations," shows the distribution of 3,000 social service organizations by tract identified in the census of nonprofit organizations undertaken in 1989 by the Nonprofit Coordinating Committee. It shows that the largest number of such organizations is in Manhattan, even though it has fewer social problems. Outside Manhattan, such organizations are much less numerous,

MAP 31
Infant Deaths Per 1,000 Live Births, 1990

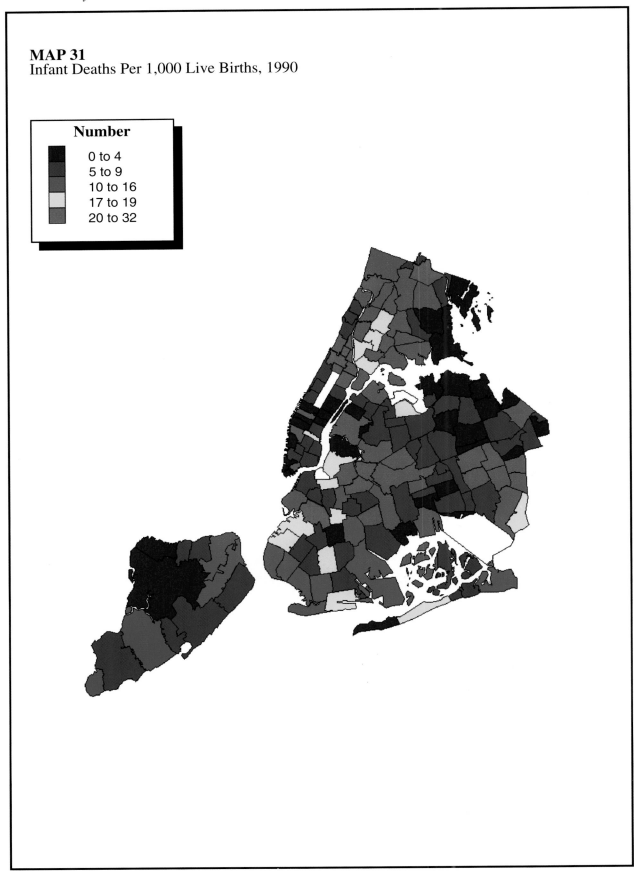

Number

0 to 4
5 to 9
10 to 16
17 to 19
20 to 32

MAP 32
Low Birth Weight Relative to Live Births, 1990

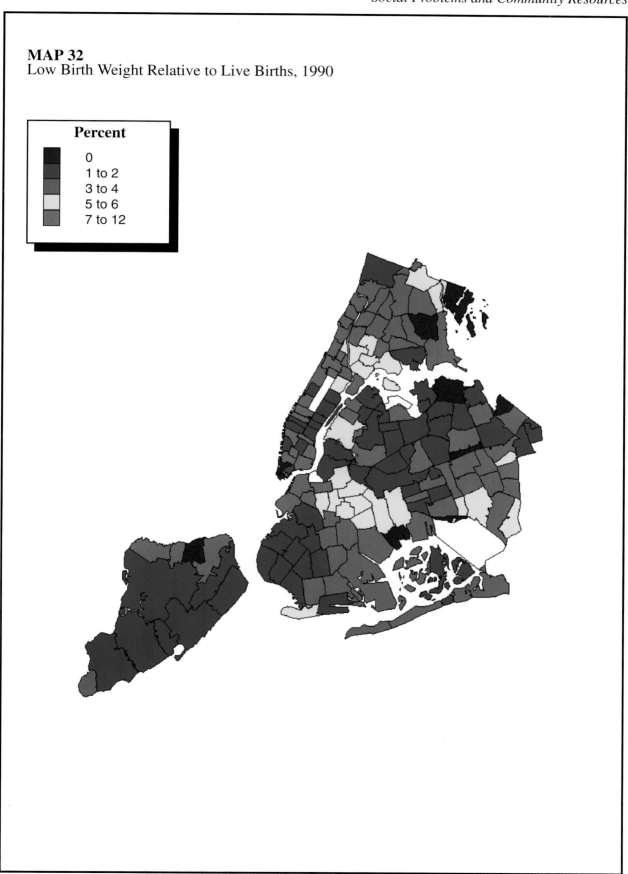

Percent

0
1 to 2
3 to 4
5 to 6
7 to 12

MAP 33
AIDS Deaths in 1990

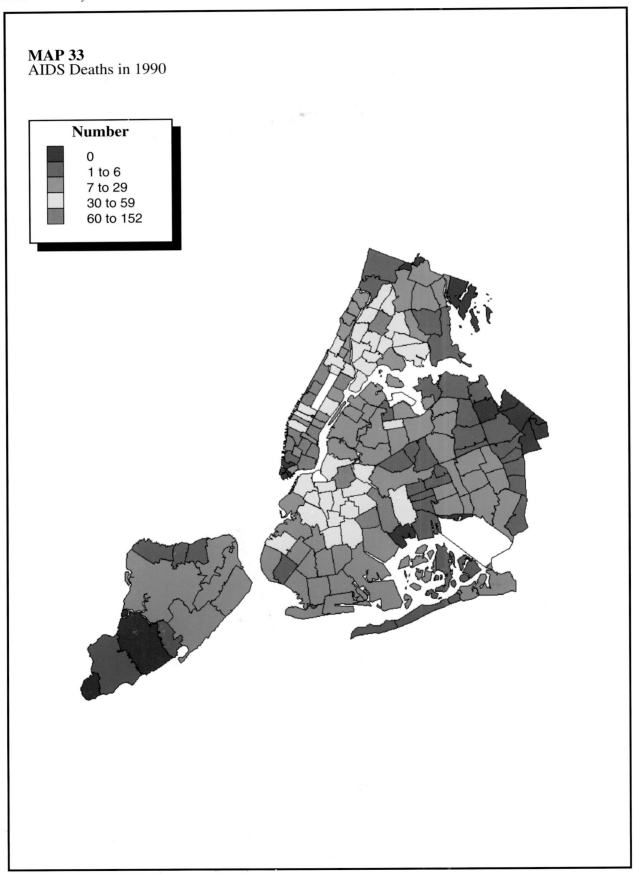

Number

0
1 to 6
7 to 29
30 to 59
60 to 152

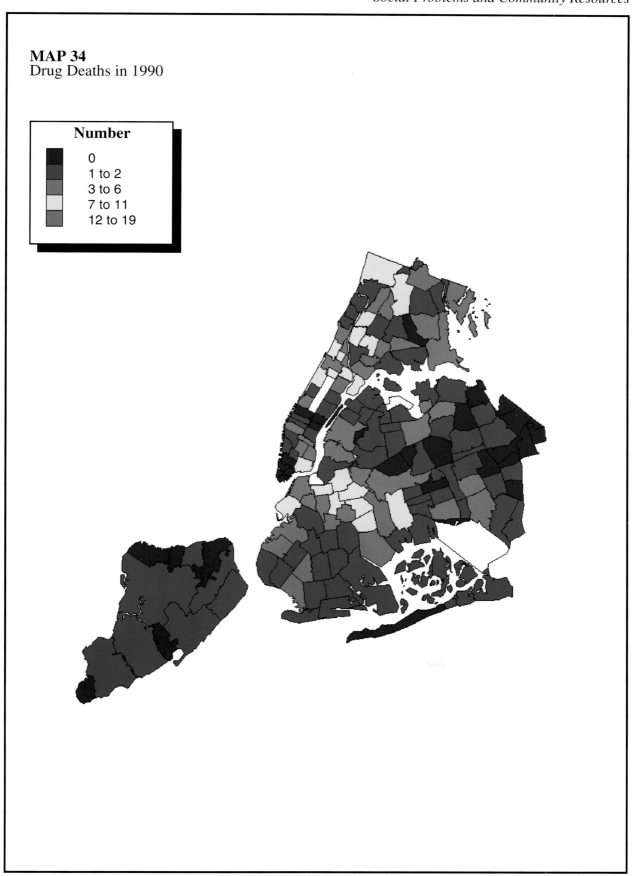

MAP 34
Drug Deaths in 1990

Number
0
1 to 2
3 to 6
7 to 11
12 to 19

MAP 35
Suicides in 1990

Number

0
1
2 to 4
5 to 9
10 to 20

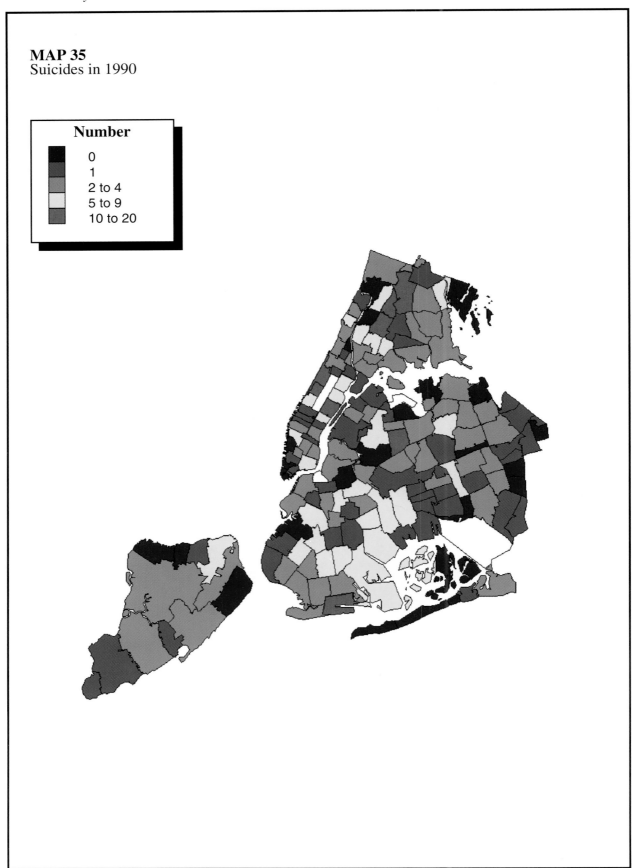

MAP 36
Homicides in 1990

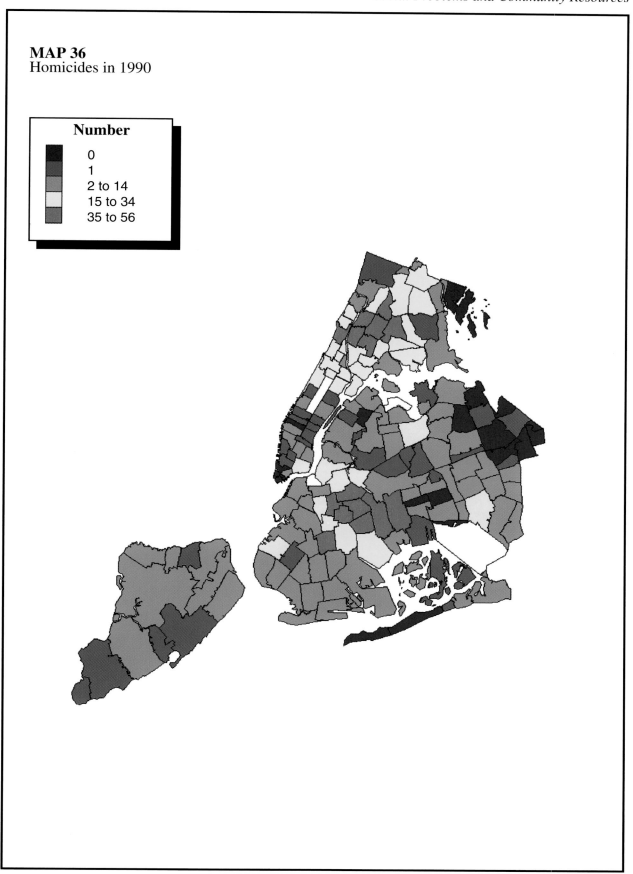

Number
0
1
2 to 14
15 to 34
35 to 56

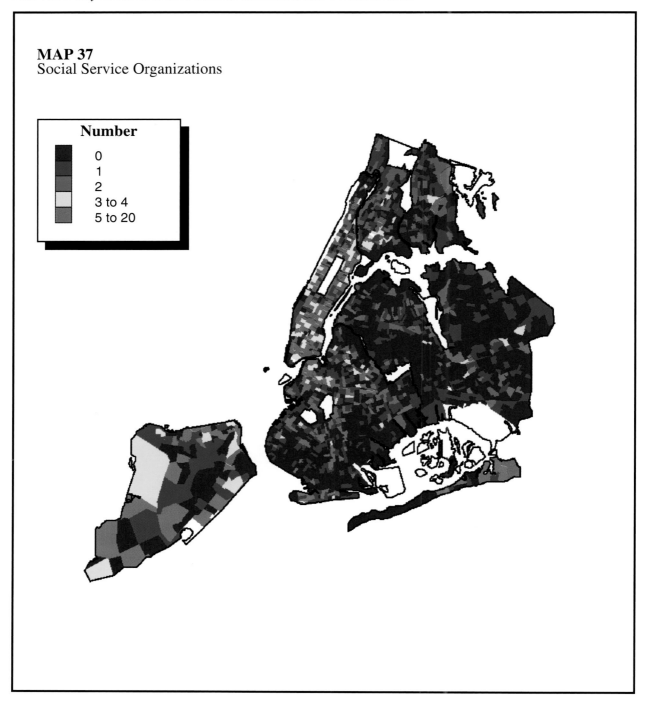

MAP 37
Social Service Organizations

Number

	0
	1
	2
	3 to 4
	5 to 20

although they do tend to be concentrated in areas with the greatest need. As Map 38, "Churches and Religious Organizations," shows, religious organizations are much more widely diffused throughout the city.

City government has also invested heavily to upgrade the low- and moderate-rent housing supply in poor neighborhoods. Map 39, "Publicly Assisted Housing Units, 1978–1989," shows the total number of units constructed or rehabilitated during the 1980s by the various programs of the Housing

MAP 38
Churches and Religious Organizations

Number

- 0
- 1 to 2
- 3 to 5
- 6 to 9
- 10 to 53

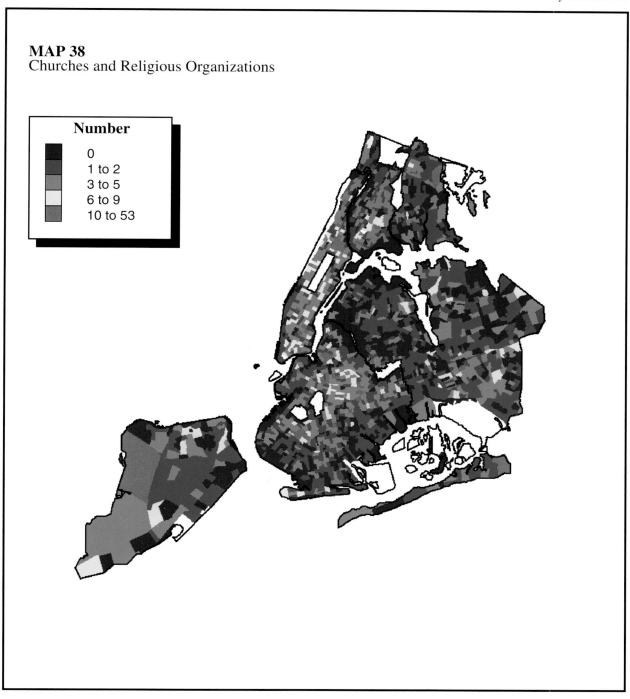

Preservation and Development Department (HPD) by community board. Most were built in the South Bronx and central Harlem. HPD constructed almost half its total units in the South Bronx, including many units for homeless families. These neighborhoods have experienced severe poverty and disinvestment and undoubtedly needed this investment, but concern has been expressed over the wisdom of concentrating so many formerly homeless families in one part of the city.

MAP 39
Publicly Assisted Housing Units, 1978–1989

Unit

0
1 to 19
20 to 399
400 to 999
1,000 to 3,519

Section III

Political Participation

ELIGIBILITY, REGISTRATION, AND THE RACIAL COMPOSITION OF THE ELECTORATE

While the composition of New York City's overall population changed a great deal in the 1980s, the makeup of its electorate changed much more slowly. Two kinds of factors affect the relation between importance in the population and importance in the electorate: eligibility and degree of political mobilization. Age and citizenship determine eligibility. As the previous discussion has shown, a far larger proportion of New York City's white population are voting-age citizens than is true of its black, Latino, and Asian population, in that order. (According to the 1990 Census, almost half the city's native-born blacks are less than 18 years old!) Appendix Table 5 shows the dimensions of these differences.

One important aspect of this table is that the new immigrant groups have not yet become an important force in New York City's politics even though they are reshaping its neighborhoods and industries. Note the large drop-off between the Latino and Asian percentage of the overall population and their percentage among voting-age citizens. Moreover, the great diversity of the immigrant population suggests that they will not be a cohesive force when they ultimately become citizens and register to vote. Like the population as a whole, they are divided by differences of race, religion, and political outlook.

Even among those who are eligible to vote, members of different groups vary considerably in terms of whether they will register and actually cast a ballot. Among the factors that influence political mobilization are the political traditions and organization of a community, the income and education of its members, whether it has attractive candidates for whom to vote, and how strongly it feels about the issues being raised in politics. White liberals (many of whom are Jewish), more traditional Jews living in the outer boroughs, and the native-born black population have generally been the most politically active and involved groups during the 1980s, followed by white Catholics and Latinos.

Partisan factors also shape political outcomes. The registration figures suggest that New York is a one party town. In 1989, 69 percent of all registered voters were Democrats; only 14 percent were Republicans. Perhaps indicating disaffection with both these parties, independent voters (15 percent) outnumbered Republicans. The minuscule Conservative, Liberal, and Right To Life parties are not mass parties but rather ballot lines that their leaders use to influence the larger parties and take advantage of divisions within them.

Most electoral contests are decided in Democratic primaries. Even people who might wish to register as Republicans have an incentive to register as Democrats. While only 14 percent of New York's voters are registered Republicans, New York City voters typically give Republican presidential candidates about 35 percent of the vote in general elections. Even assuming that all registered Republicans vote for their nominee, and assuming that Republicans, Independents, and Democrats turn out in equal proportions, we can conclude that as many as one-fourth of the registered Democrats vote consistently for Republican presidential candidates and might be termed "constructive Republicans."

MAP 40
Predominant Ethnic Group by AD, 1989

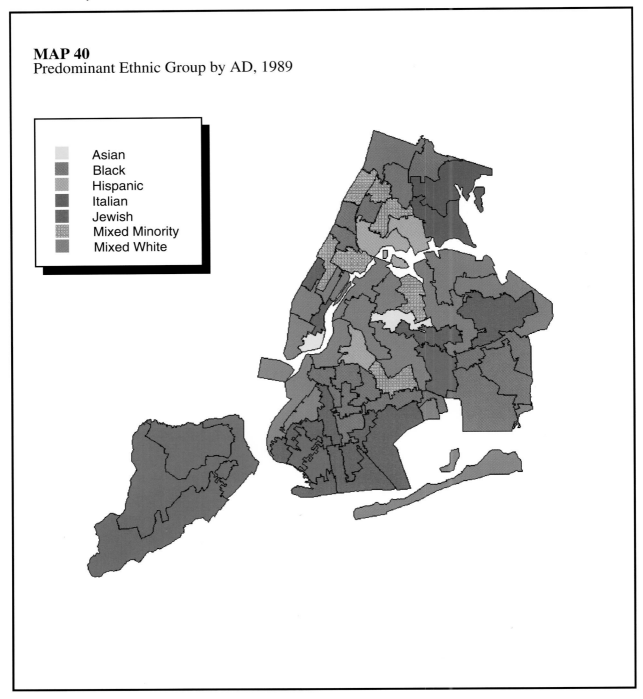

Asian
Black
Hispanic
Italian
Jewish
Mixed Minority
Mixed White

The party enrollment maps show where each party affiliation has its strongest social base. Map 40, "Predominant Ethnic Group by AD," identifies the largest ethnic group in each of 60 Assembly Districts (ADs) into which the city's political geography was divided between 1982 and 1992. (ADs are the basic building blocks of political parties in New York State; each has male and female District Leaders and one or more political clubs that organize party activities.) Map 41, "Democratic Registration by AD, 1989,"

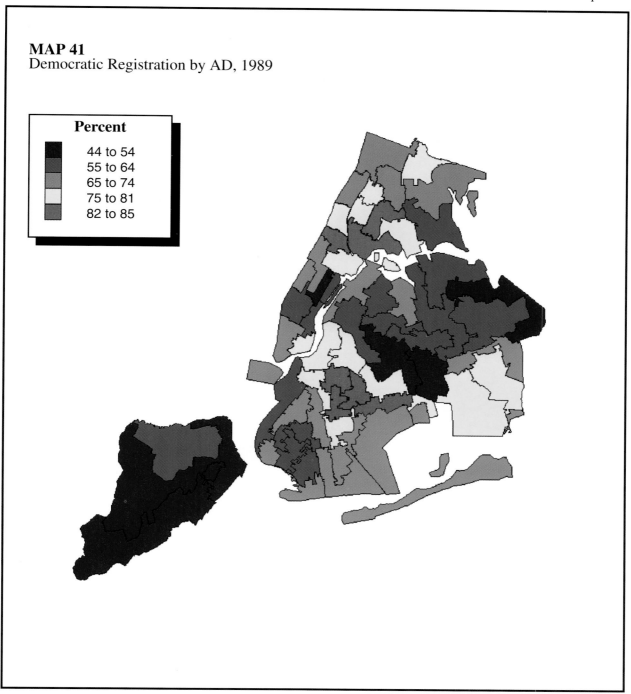

MAP 41
Democratic Registration by AD, 1989

Percent

44 to 54
55 to 64
65 to 74
75 to 81
82 to 85

shows Democrats make up the highest percentage of Democrats (red and yellow) in ADs where blacks and Puerto Ricans predominate. The middle category (light blue), 65–74 percent Democratic, includes liberal white areas such as the Upper West Side, the Village, and Park Slope, as well as outer borough Jewish areas such as the Brooklyn shore communities east of Ocean Parkway. The better-off Queens Jewish neighborhoods such as Forest Hills are less likely to be Democratic. Immigrant Latino areas also

MAP 42
Republican Registration by AD, 1989

Percent

3 to 4
5 to 9
10 to 16
17 to 24
25 to 33

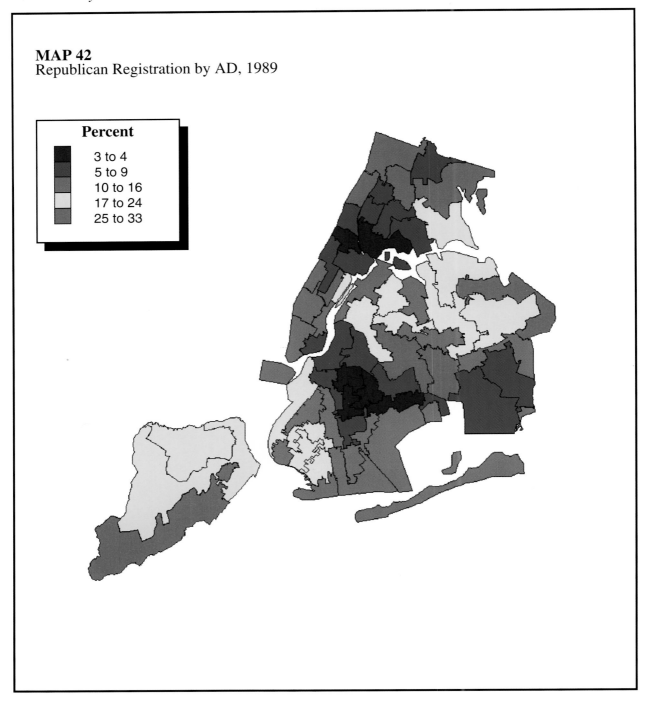

have lower rates of Democratic registration than do ADs where Puerto Ricans are the largest Latino group.

Strongly Republican areas form a mirror image to Democrats, as Map 42, "Republican Registration by AD, 1989," shows. The most strongly Republican districts (in red) include the Protestant Upper East Side, the Italian and Irish Catholic South Shore of Staten Island, and the white Catholic upper-income part of Queens along the Nassau border. In general, the white Catholic and Protestant areas of the

MAP 43
Independent Registration by AD, 1989

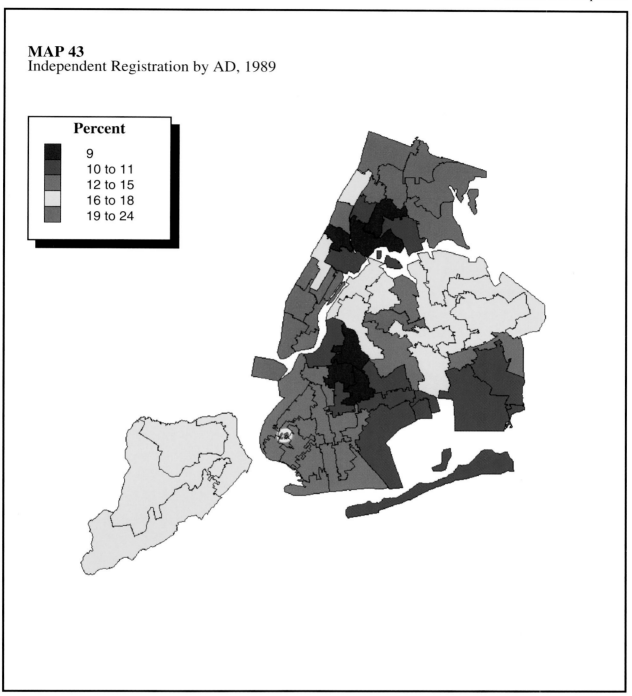

Percent
9
10 to 11
12 to 15
16 to 18
19 to 24

city are the most likely to be registered as Republicans. Independents are centered in the upper-income white ADs of Manhattan and spread through the other middle class white areas, as Map 43, "Independent Registration by AD, 1989," shows.

These patterns demonstrate that blacks, Latinos, liberal whites (many of whom may be Jewish), and more traditional Jews living outside Manhattan are most likely to register as Democrats, in that order. Least likely to register and vote Democratic are white

Anglo-Saxon Protestants, white Catholics, and Asians. While factors related to eligibility and political mobilization favor whites over blacks and Latinos in terms of who can cast a ballot, partisan factors cut the other way because minorities are more likely to register Democratic. To the extent that Democratic primaries are more important than general elections, and to the extent that blacks and Latinos are more likely than whites to register as Democrats, the Democratic partisan leaning of New York City enhances the impact of minorities on electoral outcomes. As Appendix Table 5 shows, once all these factors are taken into account, whites retain a slight majority even in the Democratic primary electorate, blacks are better represented than in the population as a whole, and Latinos and Asians remain highly underrepresented.

THE SHIFTING BASE OF DEMOCRATIC REGISTRATION

The city's black and Latino populations began the decade of the 1980s much less well represented in the potential electorate than in the population as a whole. Causes of this low rate of registration included the practices of those elected to citywide office, who had little interest in mobilizing more minority voters or presenting them with attractive minority candidates at the top of their ballots, the poverty and low education of the minority communities, and the fragmentation of their leadership. African Americans were able to change important aspects of this situation during the 1980s, but Latinos have not made as much progress on the long march to full political representation.

The voter registration campaigns of the early 1980s, the mobilizing effect of the Jesse Jackson presidential primary campaigns in 1984 and 1988, and the 1989 Dinkins campaign led to a large absolute and relative increase in black registration and turnout over the decade. These efforts had a smaller impact on Latino political registration, and particularly on Latino turnout, in part because few Latino candidates ran for the citywide offices at the top of the ballot. (In 1985, three Latinos ran for City Council President and raised Latino turnout in that race.) While Latinos gradually became more favorable toward black candidates like Jackson and Dinkins, these candidacies did not produce increases in Latino turnout. Indeed, until the 1988 Jackson campaign and the 1989 Dinkins campaign, Latinos and blacks exhibited little cross-support for each other's candidates against white opponents.

Map 44, "Ratio of Registered Voters to Voting-Age Population, 1989," shows what percentage of the voting-age population was registered in 1989. The highest levels were attained in high income white ADs, both in Democratic-leaning areas such as the Upper West Side and Republican-leaning areas such as the East Side and Staten Island's South Shore. Above-average rates have also been achieved in the predominantly black ADs in Harlem, the South Bronx, central Brooklyn, and southeast Queens. More noteworthy are areas where rates are low: not only in Latino, West Indian, or Asian immigrant zones like Washington Heights, Crown Heights, or Jackson Heights, but also in the lower middle class white ethnic enclaves of Bensonhurst,

MAP 44
Ratio of Registered Voters to Voting-Age Population, 1989

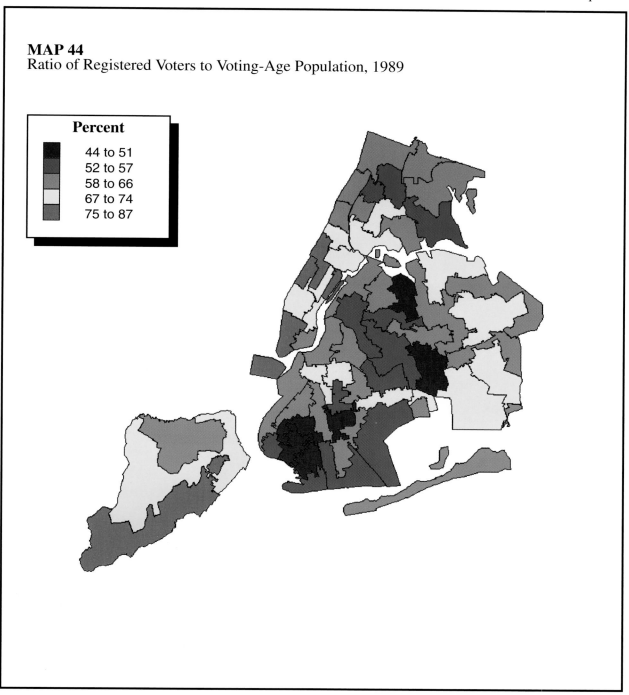

Percent

44 to 51
52 to 57
58 to 66
67 to 74
75 to 87

Midwood, Canarsie, Flatlands, Astoria, Woodside, and Richmond Hill.

Chart 2 shows that registration is cyclical. New registrants build up the rolls as a presidential election year approaches, while the Board of Elections annually purges those who have failed to vote within the previous four years or who have moved. (In 1989, a lawsuit prevented the Board from purging 311,000 voters who had not voted in four years; 68,000 voters who moved were purged, however.) Registration thus peaks in the year

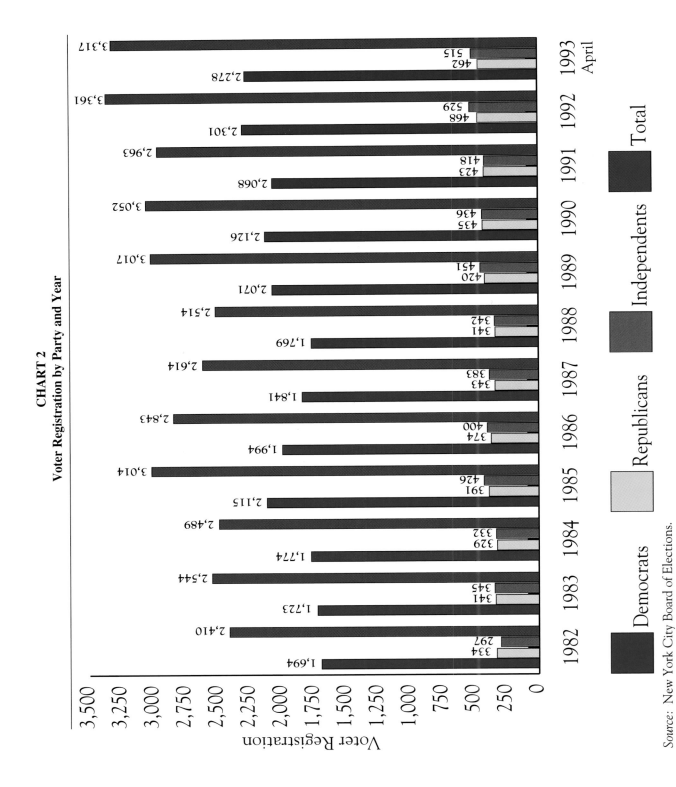

CHART 2
Voter Registration by Party and Year

Voter Registration (y-axis): 3,500 / 3,250 / 3,000 / 2,750 / 2,500 / 2,250 / 2,000 / 1,750 / 1,500 / 1,250 / 1,000 / 750 / 500 / 250 / 0

Years (x-axis): 1982 1983 1984 1985 1986 1987 1988 1989 1990 1991 1992 1993 April

Legend: Democrats | Republicans | Independents | Total

Year	Democrats	Republicans	Independents	Total
1982	1,694	334	297	2,410
1983	1,723	341	345	2,544
1984	1,774	329	332	2,489
1985	2,115	391	426	3,014
1986	1,994	374	400	2,843
1987	1,841	343	383	2,614
1988	1,769	341	342	2,514
1989	2,071	420	451	3,017
1990	2,126	435	436	3,052
1991	2,068	423	418	2,963
1992	2,301	468	529	3,361
1993 April	2,278	462	515	3,317

Source: New York City Board of Elections.

after a presidential election, which draws the most registrants and voters, and then declines for several years before the next presidential election upswing. Over the last several decades, these registration peaks declined about 20 percent, but since 1980 they have edged up slightly.

As the previous discussion of "constructive Republicans" suggests, New York City actually has two quite different electorates. From the state and national perspective, the two million or more who vote in presidential and gubernatorial general elections are the most important. This large and broad electorate gives Republican candidates more support than registration numbers alone might suggest. From the perspective of who will win elections in New York City, however, a second far smaller electorate is decisive: the 700,000 voters who participate in Democratic primaries. Since 1930, only two Republicans have won the mayoralty: Fiorello La Guardia and John V. Lindsay. Those who seek to capture city hall must thus make sure that they can build a majority within the Democratic Party. For those who aspired to elect an African-American mayor, this meant concentrating on enrolling more black and Latino voters.

Between 1982 and 1985, voter registration drives among blacks and Latinos succeeded in increasing Democratic registration and in changing its balance toward minorities and white liberals, as Map 45, "Gain in Democratic Registration, 1982–1985," shows. The white ethnic areas of southern Brooklyn and Queens showed the smallest increase. Between 1985 and 1988, however, Democratic Party registration

declined by 385,000 voters. The map of these losses, Map 46, "Loss in Democratic Registration, 1985–1988," shows that these losses were deepest in the white ethnic areas of southern Brooklyn and eastern Queens. Some Latino and black ADs showed declines, but others, especially in Flatbush and southeast Queens, showed gains. The liberal white areas of Manhattan had the strongest gains. Thus the center of gravity among registered Democrats continued to shift. (In this period, Republicans also gained in their traditional strongholds, such as Staten Island and the East Side, and made some inroads in southern Brooklyn and the white middle class parts of Queens.)

In 1988 and 1989, events hastened this process. New voter registration drives for the 1988 Jackson presidential primary campaign and David Dinkins's run for the mayoralty in 1989 enrolled large numbers of new voters. The city's Voter Assistance Program, Countdown '88, HumanSERVE, and the Commonwealth of Puerto Rico all conducted drives. By early 1989, this boosted the total registration by 500,000 voters. Map 47, "Gain in Democratic Registration, 1988–1989," shows, however, that these gains had a different geography than those in 1982–1985. The registration campaigns recovered some of the previous losses in black and Latino ADs, but the greatest gains occurred on the West Side of Manhattan, Downtown, and Brownstone Brooklyn, all areas where liberal whites predominate.

The overall result between 1982 and 1989 was thus a fairly substantial growth of black and Latino Democrats and a substantial shift among white Democrats in favor of the

MAP 45
Gain in Democratic Registration, 1982–1985

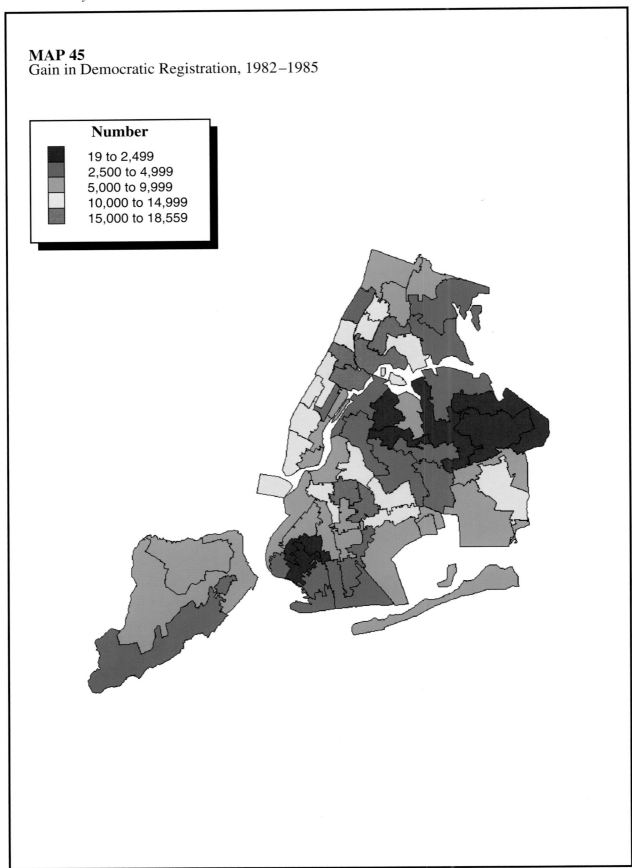

Number

19 to 2,499
2,500 to 4,999
5,000 to 9,999
10,000 to 14,999
15,000 to 18,559

MAP 46
Loss in Democratic Registration, 1985–1988

Number

- -4,404 to -2,851
- -2,850 to -1,501
- -1,500 to 0
- 1 to 2,499
- 2,500 to 5,529

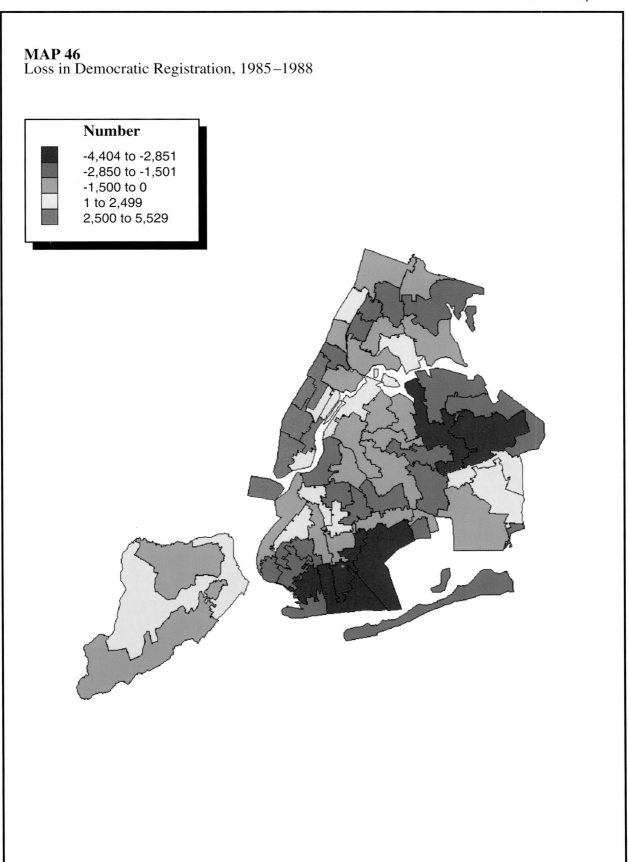

MAP 47
Gain in Democratic Registration, 1988–1989

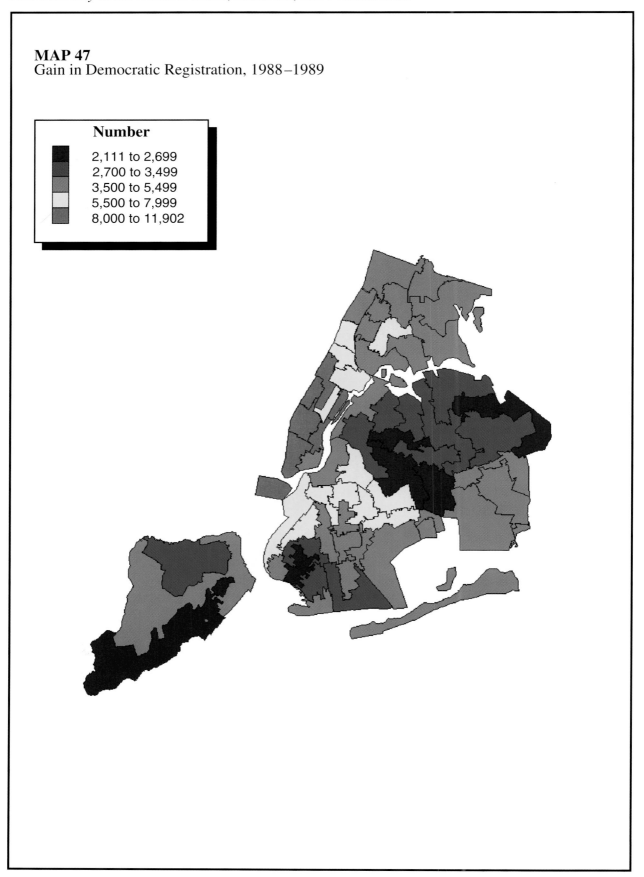

Number

2,111 to 2,699
2,700 to 3,499
3,500 to 5,499
5,500 to 7,999
8,000 to 11,902

liberal Upper West Side and Village Manhattan ADs and against the more conservative white Catholic and Jewish ADs of southern Brooklyn and central Queens. This undermined the base of support that Edward I. Koch, first elected mayor in 1977, counted on for support and opened the way for David Dinkins's challenge in the 1989 Democratic mayoral primary. The strongly Democratic partisan leanings of blacks, their high rate of turnout, and the importance of the Democratic vote in citywide elections helped to focus the electoral power of black voters. (The first factor had a small positive effect for Latinos as well but not enough to offset their low registration and turnout rates.) This helped to offset the advantages of age, citizenship, and income enjoyed by white voters and to ensure that candidates would have to address the concerns of the city's less well-off residents.

THE GENERAL ELECTORATE: THE 1988 PRESIDENTIAL CAMPAIGN

People who vote in presidential general elections every four years make up the largest and broadest electorate in New York City as in the rest of the nation. In 1984, 2.3 million (76.9 percent) of New York City's registered voters cast ballots. Due to the city's population decline in the 1970s, this number was lower than was typical in the 1960s, when more than 3 million voted. This was an improvement of 300,000 over 1980, however. In 1988, the downward slide continued, as only 2.04 million people voted. Turnout declined to 69.9 percent of those registered, matching the low points of 1972 and 1980.

Ronald Reagan got 38.9 percent of the vote in 1984, George Bush, 33.3 percent in 1988. Because suburban New Yorkers are roughly divided between the two parties and exurban voters are predominantly Republican, Republicans must win a large minority of the votes in the city in order to win statewide races. The Republican margin in the city in turn depends on the extent to which they can attract and mobilize the relatively conservative majority of white voters compared to the job the Democrats can do to win over and mobilize a more liberal and racially mixed set of constituencies.

Two maps give a picture of the 1988 presidential election, which in turn was representative of general elections in New York City in the 1980s. The map of turnout (Map 48, "Turnout, 1988 Presidential Election") shows that the fewest registered voters turned out to vote in black and Latino ADs while the largest percentage voted in high income areas that are the most predominantly Republican: Yorkville, Riverdale, Little Neck, and the South Shore of Staten Island. The Democratic candidate in this race, Michael Dukakis, simply did not mobilize the most Democratic ADs.

Bush won a majority of the vote on the East Side, the relatively white Catholic ADs of Staten Island, Bensonhurst, and southwestern Queens, and the strongly orthodox Jewish neighborhood of Borough Park. He also did better than his citywide average in the Jewish ADs of southern Brooklyn and northeastern Queens. Bush did worst in black ADs and the more liberal parts of the city, including the white West Side of Manhattan and all the black and Latino areas of the city.

MAP 48
Turnout, 1988 Presidential Election

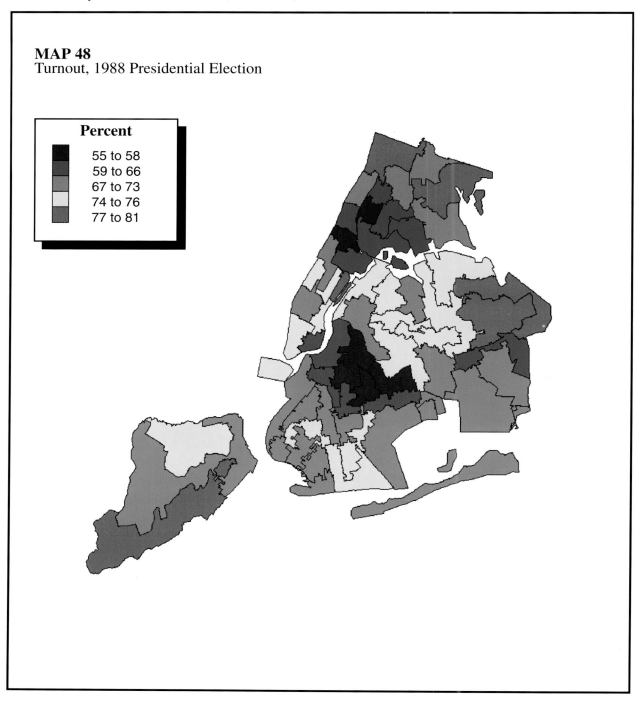

Percent

55 to 58
59 to 66
67 to 73
74 to 76
77 to 81

Bush received 5 percentage points less support than Reagan had in 1984. This slippage occurred in Astoria, where New York's Greek community is concentrated, the two Puerto Rican ADs along the Brooklyn side of the Brooklyn/Queens border in Bushwick, and in other lower middle class white Catholic areas of the city.

THE DEMOCRATIC PRIMARY ELECTORATE, THE KOCH COALITION, AND THE AFRICAN-AMERICAN ASCENT TO POWER

In addition to his base among middle class Jewish and white Catholic residents of the outer boroughs, Mayor Edward I. Koch sought to bring into his electoral coalition the independents and Republicans who were drawn toward Presidents Reagan and Bush in the presidential general elections of the 1980s. However, to secure his hold on power, he had to build solid majorities within the smaller and more liberal Democratic primary electorate, where minorities made up a larger fraction of the vote.

Koch was first elected in 1977 on the basis of his liberal record as a congressman who represented Greenwich Village. While he distinguished himself from more liberal candidates like Bella Abzug in the 1977 primaries by stressing his positions in favor of the death penalty and against municipal unions and "povertycrats," he relied on liberal, black, and Latino votes to gain office in the 1977 general election. However, once in office, he redefined his electoral and governing coalition in a more conservative direction, winning reelection in 1981 on this basis. Although he lost the Democratic gubernatorial primary in 1982 to Mario Cuomo, he rebuilt his position within the city mayoral Democratic primary electorate in 1985. This election gives a good picture of the Koch electoral coalition at its moment of maximum strength.

The geography of Mayor Koch's overwhelming 1985 primary victory against a white liberal and an African-American challenger may be seen in Map 49, "Koch Vote, 1985 Democratic Primary." It shows that the only ADs in which Koch did not win the 40 percent he needed to avoid a run-off primary were the African-American areas of Harlem, central Brooklyn, and southeast Queens. His strongest support came from the heavily Jewish ADs of Borough Park, the Ocean Parkway-Kings Highway, Marine Park, and Canarsie sections of southern Brooklyn, the Kew Gardens-Forest Hills area of Queens, and the Irish and Italian Catholic South Shore of Staten Island. Support was soft for Koch in the more liberal parts of Manhattan like the Upper West Side and the Village, but he still won 40 percent or more of the vote. Thus he combined, as Table 2 shows, extremely strong support from his core outer borough Jewish and Italian Catholic constituencies with a majority from white liberals and Latinos and even a sizeable minority of black voters.

In contrast to the 1984 Jackson primary, the black candidate who ran against Mayor Koch in the 1985 Democratic mayoral primary, Herman D. "Denny" Farrell, did not galvanize black voters. Indeed, Map 50, "Farrell Vote Compared to Jackson Vote, 1985 and 1984 Democratic Primaries," shows that black ADs gave him a level of support that was 56 percentage points lower than the percentage they gave Jesse Jackson in 1984. (Table 2 shows that the black ADs had the lowest turnout in 1985.) The highest turnout ADs ranged from Brighton Beach and the white part of Flatbush in Brooklyn to Stuyvesant Town in Manhattan and to Washington Heights and Co-op City in the Bronx. These areas have large populations of older, lower middle class Jews living in apartment

MAP 49
Koch Vote, 1985 Democratic Primary

Percent

33 to 39
40 to 54
55 to 74
75 to 79
80 to 85

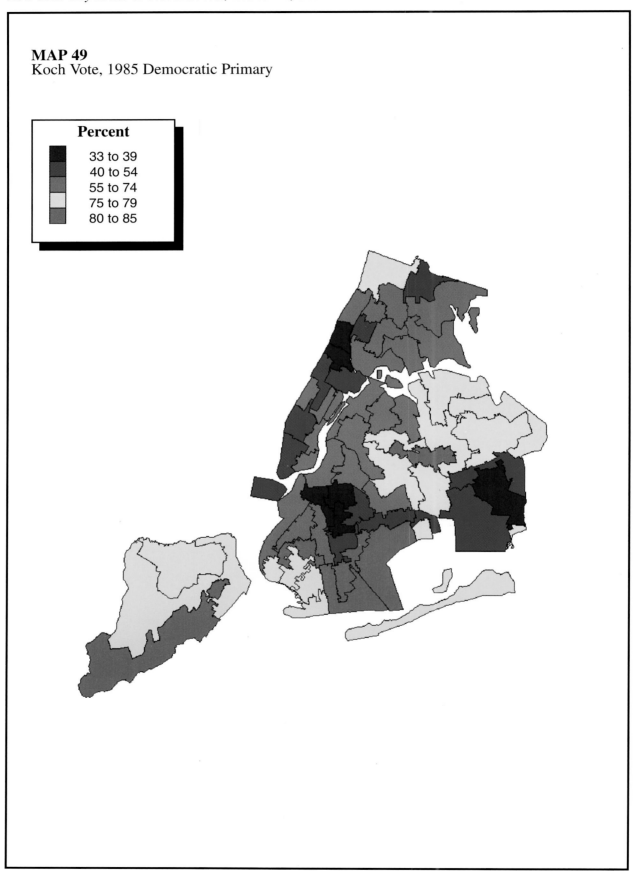

TABLE 2
Support for Mayor Koch, 1985 and 1989 Democratic Primaries by AD Type

AD Type	1985			1989			Difference	
	Votes	Koch	Turnout	Votes	Koch	Turnout	Koch	Turnout
Black	129,464	41.0	26.8	264,072	10.3	70.9	-30.7	44.1
Mixed minority	54,131	58.2	30.6	82,042	26.8	60.3	-31.4	29.7
Latino	55,353	62.4	31.6	79,194	31.8	56.6	-30.6	25.0
Liberal	147,000	59.2	36.7	212,904	46.0	43.1	-13.2	6.4
Catholic	122,456	73.6	30.9	173,059	61.4	36.4	-12.2	5.5
Outer borough Jewish	180,150	77.6	37.4	248,916	67.2	48.7	-10.4	11.3
Total	688,554	63.3	32.6	1,060,205	42.0	49.9	-21.3	17.3

Source: New York City Board of Elections.

Notes: AD stands for Assembly District. Turnout is the percentage of votes cast by registered voters. Decimal numbers are percentages. This table is reproduced by permission of the publisher, from John H. Mollenkopf's *A Phoenix in the Ashes* (Princeton, NJ: Princeton University Press, 1992).

buildings, who formed the core of Mayor Koch's constituency. The contrast between Farrell's performance in 1985 and Jackson's in 1984 shows how a candidate's magnetism, not just his race, can influence voter mobilization.

Although Jesse Jackson's 1988 presidential campaign did not produce the same increase in black and Latino registration that his 1984 campaign did, it produced a surge of turnout among black voters in the 1988 presidential primary, which drew 240,000 more voters than did the 1985 mayoral primary. The great bulk of this surge occurred in the areas that were least likely to support Mayor Koch in 1985. As we have seen, the registration shifts among white Democrats from 1985 to 1989 also tended to undercut the strength of Mayor Koch's core constituencies.

Map 51, "Jackson Vote, 1988 Democratic Primary," shows that Jesse Jackson not only won nine out of ten black voters, he attracted substantial numbers of Latino voters to a black candidate for the first time. Indeed, he won well more than a majority of the vote in

all the ADs in which Latino voters were a large presence. Finally, he won more than 20 percent, but less than a majority, of the vote in all the white liberal ADs. This showing improved greatly on Farrell's showing in 1985 and on his own previous race in 1984. More important, it dramatically improved turnout in black ADs. Unlike the 1988 presidential general election, in which Map 48 showed that black, Latino, and liberal areas had the lowest turnout, the 1988 primary race mobilized these constituencies.

This set the stage for the 1989 Democratic mayoral primary, which pitted Mayor Edward I. Koch, regarded as a highly skilled and powerful politician but one who was wounded by the municipal scandals that began to unfold in 1986, against David N. Dinkins, the African-American borough president of Manhattan, and two capable and well-funded Jewish candidates, City Comptroller Harrison "Jay" Goldin and former Metropolitan Transportation Authority head Richard Ravitch.

MAP 50
Farrell Vote Compared to Jackson Vote, 1985 and 1984 Democratic Primaries

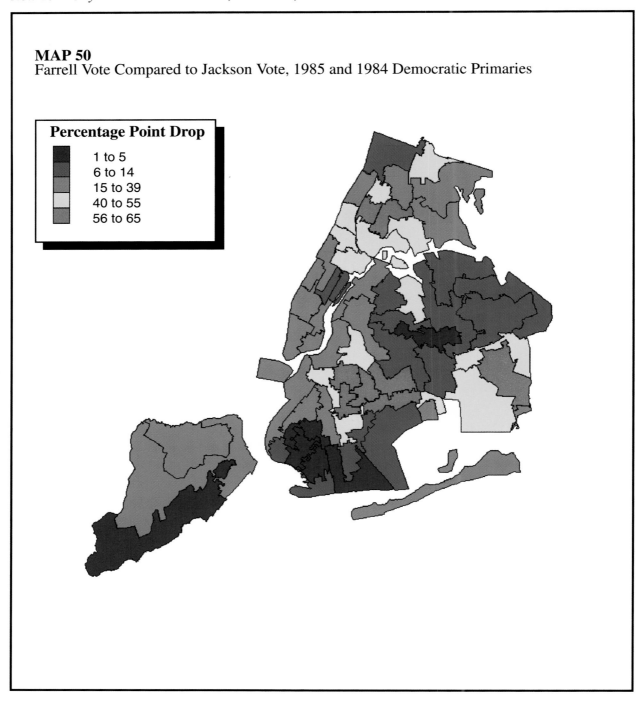

Percentage Point Drop

1 to 5
6 to 14
15 to 39
40 to 55
56 to 65

Koch had clearly lost ground from his 1985 high point, but it remained to be seen whether Dinkins could equal Jackson's performance among black and Latino constituencies while building the necessary support among white voters. Jackson had won a 40-percent plurality in 1988 in part because white voters had not been excited about choosing Dukakis or Gore. Dinkins had to do better than 40 percent in an even more racially polarized environment than the 1988 presidential primary.

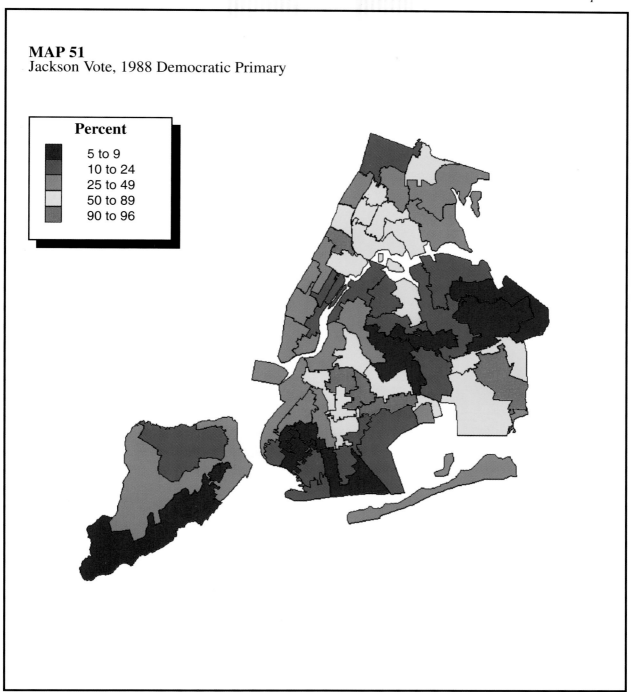

MAP 51
Jackson Vote, 1988 Democratic Primary

Percent

5 to 9
10 to 24
25 to 49
50 to 89
90 to 96

How Dinkins built his majority is shown in Map 52, "Dinkins Vote, 1989 Democratic Primary." He won overwhelming majorities in the predominantly black ADs, substantial majorities in the Latino ADs and some of the white liberal ADs, and large minorities in the other white liberal ADs and even in some white ethnic lower middle class areas like the northeast Bronx and Astoria. Map 53, "Dinkins Vote Compared to Jackson Vote, 1989 and 1988 Democratic Primaries," shows that while Dinkins did not do quite as well in

MAP 52
Dinkins Vote, 1989 Democratic Primary

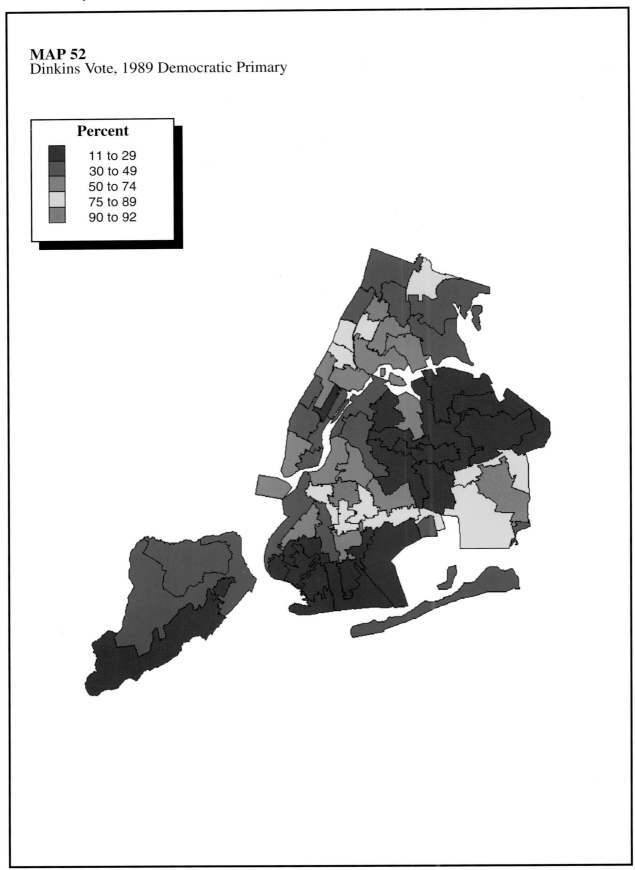

Percent

	11 to 29
	30 to 49
	50 to 74
	75 to 89
	90 to 92

MAP 53
Dinkins Vote Compared to Jackson Vote, 1989 and 1988 Democratic Primaries

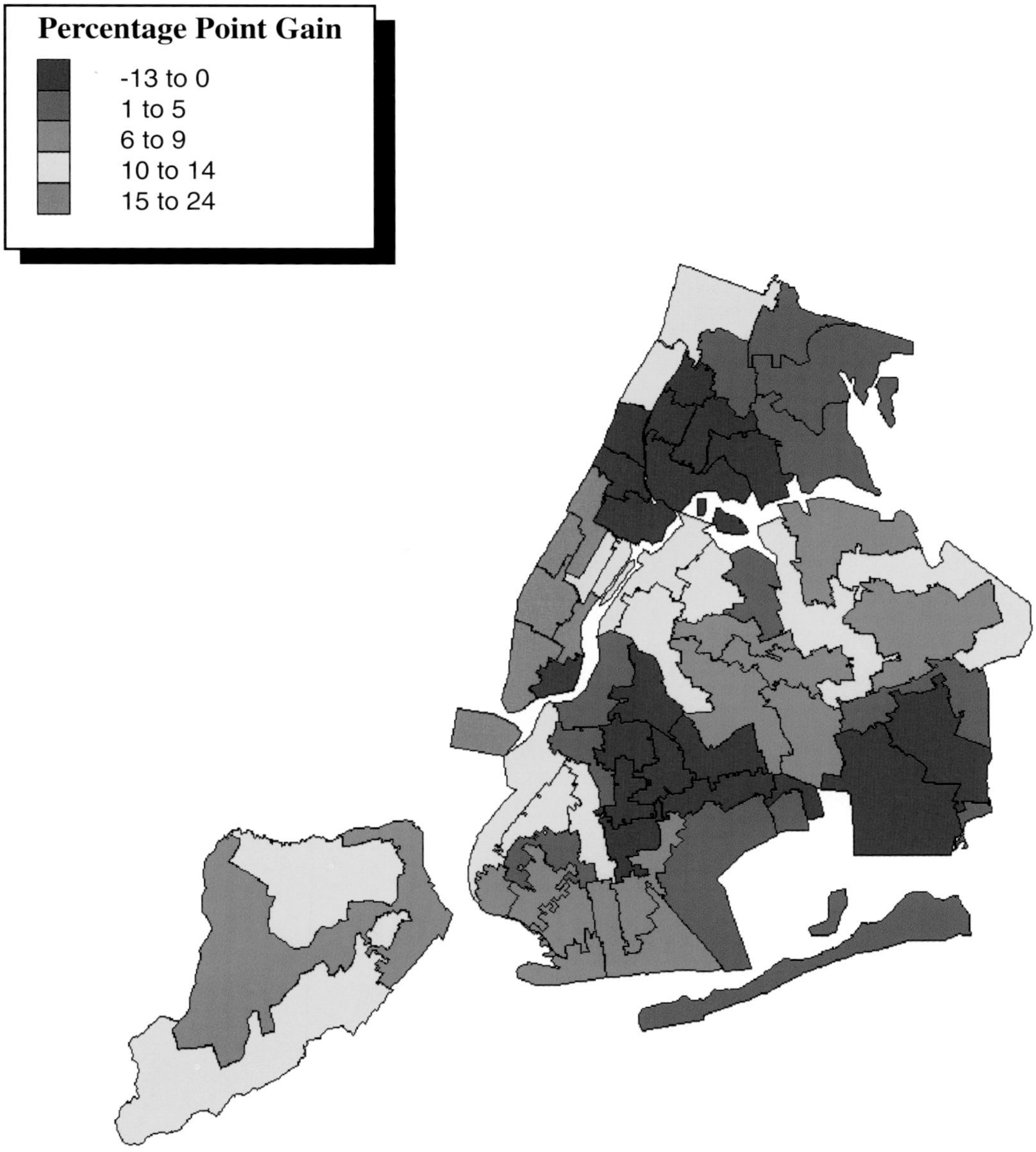

Percentage Point Gain

- -13 to 0
- 1 to 5
- 6 to 9
- 10 to 14
- 15 to 24

TABLE 3
Dinkins 1989 Performance Relative to Farrell in 1985 and Jackson in 1988

AD TYPE	NEW YORK CITY DEMOCRATIC PRIMARIES								
	1985			1988			1989		
	VOTES	FARRELL	TURNOUT	VOTES	JACKSON	TURNOUT	VOTES	DINKINS	TURNOUT
Black	129,464	32.7	26.8	227,879	88.2	48.3	264,072	84.8	70.9
Mixed minority	54,131	19.8	30.6	69,069	71.4	39.8	82,042	65.1	60.3
Latino	55,353	17.8	31.6	67,740	63.5	39.4	79,194	60.4	56.6
Liberal	147,000	6.4	36.7	188,946	27.8	44.0	212,904	44.6	43.1
Catholic	122,456	6.1	30.9	150,710	22.7	40.5	173,059	30.4	36.4
Outer borough Jewish	180,150	5.6	37.4	222,689	17.7	49.7	248,916	25.9	48.7
Total	688,554	13.0	32.6	927,060	45.3	45.0	1,060,205	50.8	49.9

Source: New York City Board of Elections.
Notes: AD stands for Assembly District. Turnout is the percentage of votes cast by registered voters. Decimal numbers are percentages. This table is reproduced by permission of the publisher, from John H. Mollenkopf's *A Phoenix in the Ashes* (Princeton, NJ: Princeton University Press, 1992).

predominantly black ADs as Jackson had a year earlier, he improved dramatically on Jackson's performance in key areas. (See also Table 3.) The most important of these were the vote-rich, high-turnout white liberal ADs of the Upper West Side, Chelsea, the Village, and Downtown neighborhoods of Manhattan where Dinkins gained 15 percentage points or more over Jackson. However, Dinkins also gained 10–15 percentage points on the East Side, the generally working-class white ethnic parts of western Queens, the mixed working-class and middle class white ethnic parts of southwest Brooklyn, and even on Staten Island.

These shifts to Dinkins were also decisive defections from Mayor Koch's 1985 electoral coalition, as Map 54, "Decline in Koch Vote, 1985 and 1989 Democratic Primaries," shows. (See also Table 2.) Only in the deeply Italian Catholic ADs of Bensonhurst did Koch hold on to the percentage he achieved in the 1985 Democratic mayoral primary. Everywhere else, voters defected, with the

strongest movement arising in the somewhat better-off parts of the South Bronx (an area of mixed black and Latino settlement) and the areas of Brooklyn settled by a mixture of Latinos, native-born African Americans, and West Indian immigrants.

While Map 54 shows that the largest and most important defections occurred in black and Latino areas, fairly heavy defections (reduction of the Koch vote by 10–25 percentage points) occurred throughout the rest of the city. Only in predominantly Jewish ADs was this defection held to less than 10 percentage points. Map 55, "Increase in Turnout, 1985 and 1989 Democratic Primaries," shows that shifts in turnout magnified the importance of these defections. Turnout grew most strongly (red and yellow) in ADs where African-American voters predominated. The only area favorable to Mayor Koch that showed a comparable level of increased mobilization was Borough Park, a heavily Orthodox Jewish AD.

MAP 54
Decline in Koch Vote, 1985 and 1989 Democratic Primaries

Percentage Points

- -39 to -34
- -33 to -26
- -25 to -13
- -12 to -6
- -5 to 1

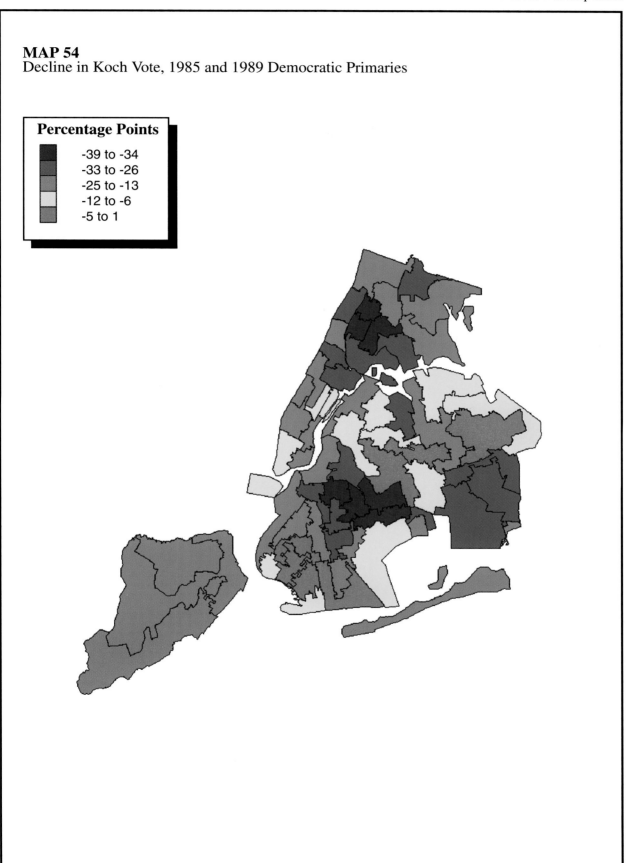

MAP 55
Increase in Turnout, 1985 and 1989 Democratic Primaries

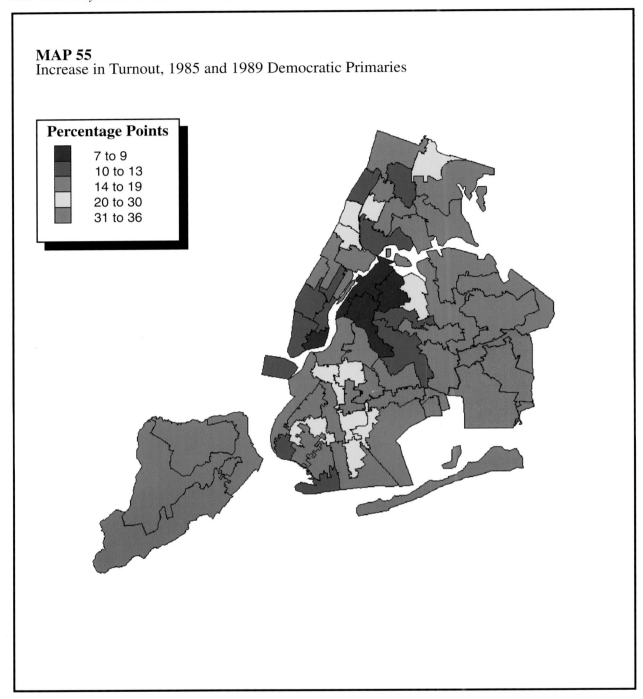

Percentage Points

7 to 9
10 to 13
14 to 19
20 to 30
31 to 36

This set the stage for one of the most unusual and interesting elections ever to take place in New York City. The previous discussion has underscored the fact that Republican mayoral candidates do not generally win citywide office. But never before had the Demo-cratic nominee for mayor been a black man. The challenge for Rudolph Giuliani, the Republican nominee in 1989, was to add significant elements of the former Koch coalition to his natural Republican base of about 35 percent in contested citywide general elec-

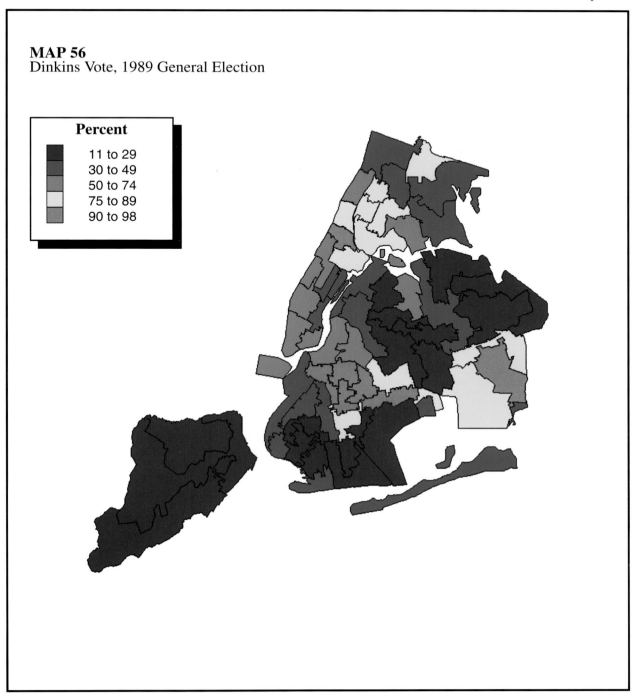

MAP 56
Dinkins Vote, 1989 General Election

Percent

11 to 29
30 to 49
50 to 74
75 to 89
90 to 98

tions. In other words, just as candidate Dinkins had to add Latinos and more conservative and less Democratic middle class Jews and white Catholics to his black and liberal white electoral base, candidate Giuliani had to add white liberals, less liberal Jewish Democrats, and Latinos to his predominantly white Catholic electoral base. Significant elements of the Koch coalition were up for grabs.

As Map 56, "Dinkins Vote, 1989 General Election," shows, Dinkins was able to win strong support from Latinos (most of whom

TABLE 4
1989 Mayoral Primary and General Elections in New York City by AD Type

	ELECTION							
	PRIMARY				GENERAL			
AD TYPE	VOTES	DINKINS	KOCH	TURNOUT	VOTES	DINKINS	GIULIANI	TURNOUT
Black	264,072	84.8	10.3	70.9	359,913	89.0	10.4	61.2
Mixed minority	82,042	65.1	26.8	60.3	116,449	76.7	22.4	52.4
Latino	79,194	60.4	31.8	56.6	116,222	73.6	25.4	53.2
Liberal	212,904	44.6	46.0	43.1	360,448	48.5	50.0	54.1
Catholic	173,059	30.4	61.4	36.4	399,359	25.8	71.9	64.5
Outer borough Jewish	248,916	25.9	67.2	48.7	430,302	29.3	68.6	63.6
Total	1,060,205	50.8	42.0	49.9	1,782,724	50.4	48.0	59.6

Source: New York City Board of Elections.
Notes: AD stands for Assembly District. Turnout is the percentage of votes cast by registered voters. Decimal numbers are percentages. This table is reproduced by permission of the publisher, from John H. Mollenkopf's *A Phoenix in the Ashes* (Princeton, NJ: Princeton University Press, 1992).

had supported Koch in the primary) while retaining enough support among liberal whites, Jews, and white Catholics to narrowly defeat the Republican nominee. (See also Table 4.) Dinkins won majorities exceeding 90 percent in all but three black ADs (those with large West Indian populations) and majorities exceeding 75 percent in the other black ADs and most Latino ADs, and majorities exceeding 50 percent in the other Latino ADs and the liberal white Manhattan ADs.

Map 57, "Giuliani Vote, 1989 General Election," presents the mirror image: the vote for Giuliani. His highest vote (exceeding 90 percent) came from the areas most heavily populated by white Catholics, including Bensonhurst, the Woodhaven-Middle Village section of Queens, and the South Shore of Staten Island. He got majority support, however, from most of the rest of the white ADs outside of Manhattan, including strong support from Jewish ADs in the outer boroughs.

Many white ethnic Democrats defected from their party's nominee, as shown in Map 58, "Giuliani Vote Compared to Bush Vote, 1989 and 1988 General Elections." The heaviest defection of normally Democratic vote in general elections, over 30 percentage points, came in Jewish ADs of Brooklyn and Queens such as Midwood, Manhattan Beach, Canarsie, Forest Hills, Kew Gardens, Rego Park, and Fresh Meadows, and white Catholic areas like Bensonhurst, Astoria, and Whitestone. A modest counter-defection of normally Republican blacks took place toward Dinkins in nine predominantly black ADs (the dark blue areas).

Several elements proved decisive in this contest, as Map 59, "Shift in Dinkins Vote, 1989 Primary and General Elections," shows. It illustrates areas where Dinkins's percentage in the general election exceeded that of the primary election. Dinkins made his largest gains in predominantly Latino ADs like El Barrio, the Lower East Side, the South Bronx,

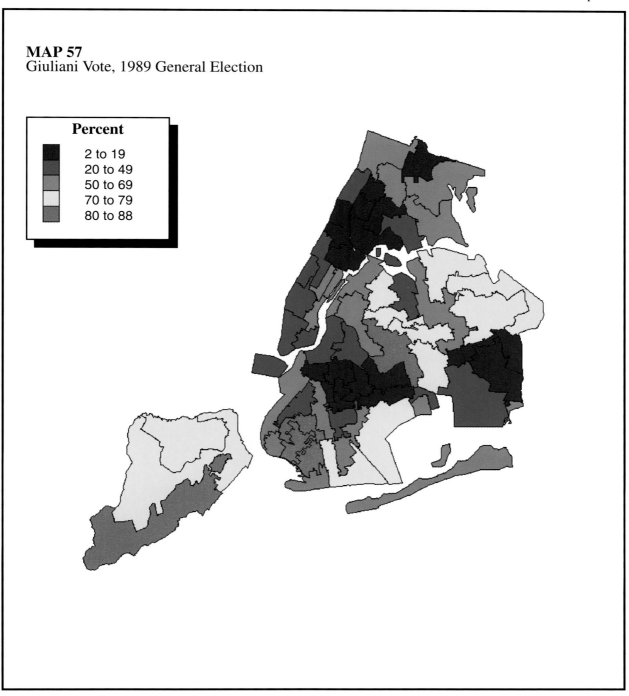

MAP 57
Giuliani Vote, 1989 General Election

Percent
2 to 19
20 to 49
50 to 69
70 to 79
80 to 88

Williamsburg-Bushwick. Gains in excess of 7 percentage points also occurred in Bushwick-East New York, northern Manhattan, and elsewhere in the Bronx. (He also improved his performance by that margin in Flatbush and Bedford-Stuyvesant.) Second, Dinkins made extensive gains on Manhattan's white liberal West Side. Finally, Dinkins made significant inroads in two largely Jewish areas, the Midwood-Kings Highway 45th AD in Brooklyn and the 28th AD containing Kew Gardens and Forest Hills in Queens. More-

MAP 58
Giuliani Vote Compared to Bush Vote, 1989 and 1988 General Elections

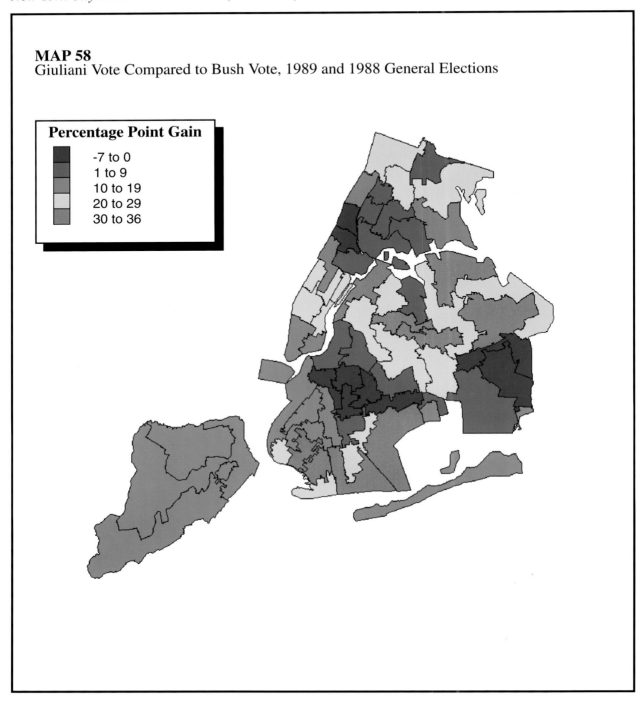

Percentage Point Gain

- -7 to 0
- 1 to 9
- 10 to 19
- 20 to 29
- 30 to 36

over, he made modest gains of up to 7 percent over his primary performance in other white middle class areas of the city. When combined with the fact that black ADs had a far higher turnout than in most past general elections, these were enough to give Dinkins a slight majority over Giuliani.

Because the mayoral election of 1993 promises to repeat many aspects of the 1989 race, it will be fascinating to watch how the balance of electoral elements changes over time. Although the change in AD boundaries

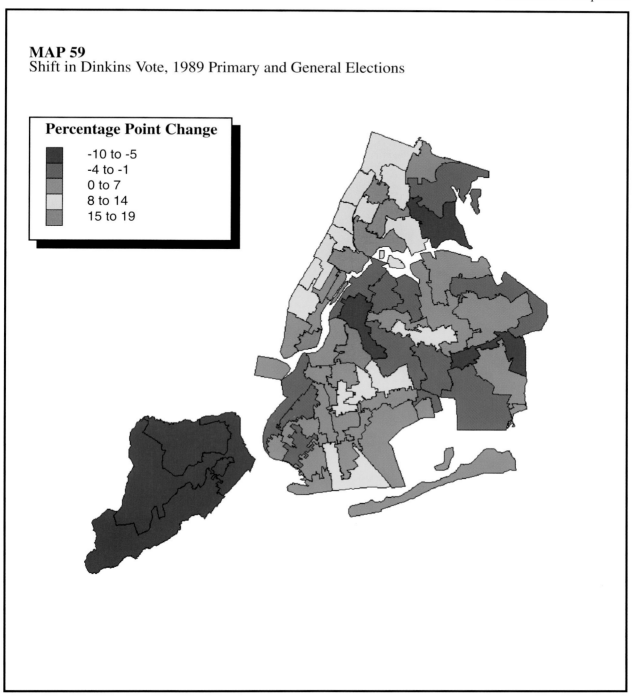

MAP 59
Shift in Dinkins Vote, 1989 Primary and General Elections

Percentage Point Change

- -10 to -5
- -4 to -1
- 0 to 7
- 8 to 14
- 15 to 19

and the renumbering and revising of election districts in 1992 makes strict comparison impossible, it appears that Democratic registration has continued to shift toward the black and Latino parts of New York City. This will favor Mayor Dinkins, although the larger issues of the relative turnout among various groups and which candidate these groups favor will ultimately determine the outcome of the 1993 elections.

Appendix

Tables

APPENDIX TABLE 1
Employment Trends by Industry of Rising Sectors in New York City: 1969, 1977, 1989
(in thousands)

SECTOR	1969	1977	1989	ANNUAL 1977–1989	PROPORTION OF SERVICE GAIN 1977–1989
Total	3,798	3,188	3,669	1.10	NA
Goods production and distribution	1,961	1,307	994	-0.96	—
Services	1,837	1,881	2,675	3.25	100.0
Financial services	466	414	531	2.36	15.9
Banking	97	118	171		
Securities	99	70	137		
Corporate services	183	228	541	11.44	42.6
Legal services	28	39	76		
Management consulting	35	22	33		
Accounting	23	21	31		
Engineering and architecture	21	16	21		
Building services	—	35	47		
Personnel services	—	27	54		
Communications, transport, and media	249	212	220	0.31	1.1
Communications	86	76	66[a]		
Advertising	39	32	39		
Publishing	70	52	61		
Entertainment, culture, and tourism	185	162	230	3.49	9.3
Restaurants and bars	123	106	131		
Hotels	34	24	34		
Legitimate theater	10	14	30		
Museums	4[b]	5	8		
Education and research	158	248	316	2.28	9.3
Elementary and secondary	151	151	184		
colleges	—	77	113		
Health and social services	198	240	350	3.82	15.0
Hospitals	104	119	139		
Other health services	47	66	100		
Social services	47[b]	55	121		
Government (noneducation)	398	377	427	1.11	6.8
Local	254	242	299		
State	38	51	56		
Federal	106	84	76		

Source: New York State Department of Labor Non-Agricultural Employment by Establishment series.

Notes: NA stands for not available. Decimal numbers are percentages. This table is reproduced by permission of the publisher, from John H. Mollenkopf's *A Phoenix in the Ashes* (Princeton, NJ: Princeton University Press, 1992).

[a]This number reflects reclassification due to the breakup of AT&T and adjustment for a labor dispute in 1989.

[b]These numbers represent estimates.

APPENDIX TABLE 2
Population Changes in New York City, 1970–1990

POPULATION	1970	1980	1990	DIFFERENCE 1980–1990
Total population	7,894,862	7,071,639	7,322,564	3.55
Non-Hispanic white population	4,972,509	3,668,945	3,163,125	-13.79
Percentage of total population	63.0	51.9	43.2	
Non-Hispanic black population	1,525,745	1,694,127	1,847,049	9.03
Native born	NA	1,300,144	1,429,543	9.95
Foreign born	NA	393,983	417,506	5.97
Hispanic population	1,278,630	1,406,024	1,783,511	26.85
Puerto Rican	846,731	860,552	896,763	4.21
Non-Puerto Rican	476,913	545,472	886,748	62.62
Non-Hispanic Asian population	115,830	300,406	489,851	63.06
Foreign-born population	1,437,058	1,670,199	2,082,931	24.71
Total households	2,836,872	2,788,530	2,819,401	1.11
Family households	2,043,765	1,757,564	1,734,908	-1.29
Married couple families	1,603,387	1,203,387	1,098,418	-8.72
Married couple families with children younger than 18	774,496	535,581	510,813	-4.62
Female-headed households	353,692	462,933	507,459	9.62
Female-headed households with children younger than 18	209,006	307,709	325,299	5.72
Nonfamily households	793,107	1,030,966	1,084,493	5.19
Average persons per household	2.74	2.49	2.54	2.00
Males in labor force	1,988,774	1,732,165	1,891,211	9.18
Percentage of males older than 16	74.1	69.5	71.1	
Females in labor force	1,355,654	1,435,533	1,695,217	18.09
Percentage of females older than 16	42.2	47.1	53.7	

Source: The 1970, 1980, 1990 U.S. Census Public Use Microdata Samples (PUMSs) files.

Notes: NA stands for not available. Decimal numbers are percentages. This table is reproduced by permission of the publisher, from John H. Mollenkopf's *A Phoenix in the Ashes* (Princeton, NJ: Princeton University Press, 1992).

NATIVE BORN	CONSTRUCTION	APPAREL	MANUFACTURING	TRANSPORT, COMMUNICATIONS, AND UTILITIES	WHOLESALE	RETAIL	RESTAURANTS
English	2.3	0.8	10.2	5.5	3.0	6.4	2.8
German	3.4	0.8	9.6	8.8	4.1	8.3	2.4
Irish	4.4	0.7	7.3	10.0	3.7	7.6	3.2
Italian	5.9	1.4	8.2	11.8	4.5	11.3	2.7
Jewish	2.0	1.5	8.6	5.6	5.4	8.5	1.8
Black	3.8	0.9	5.1	8.7	2.7	8.5	3.0
Puerto Rican	4.5	2.8	9.8	8.6	4.3	11.9	3.6
FOREIGN BORN							
Soviet	6.4	1.9	12.1	8.4	4.8	10.8	3.1
Chinese	3.0	23.8	10.0	3.9	4.0	8.1	23.5
Indian	3.4	1.8	8.2	10.1	4.4	14.9	3.4
Korean	2.9	4.5	7.0	6.0	5.7	30.4	7.0
Dominican	4.5	7.6	19.8	6.6	5.5	15.4	6.6
Colombian	6.1	5.3	15.2	8.1	3.2	10.6	8.2
Jamaican	6.2	0.7	6.3	8.5	2.3	8.4	2.8
Guyanese	4.5	3.3	10.9	7.5	4.3	11.1	2.6

Source: The 1990 U.S. Census PUMS.

Note: Rows do not add to 100 due to rounding.

TABLE 3
Group, Employed Persons, 1990
percentages)

Finance, Insurance, and Real Estate	Corporate Services	Other Services	Health	Education	Social Services	Government	Total Employed
16.0	7.9	21.8	5.4	9.2	4.9	3.0	92,211
15.6	6.3	16.5	7.0	8.6	3.9	3.9	168,826
16.2	5.2	13.2	8.6	8.8	3.6	7.0	235,627
15.8	4.3	11.5	7.2	7.7	2.6	4.6	383,214
12.8	7.7	15.2	9.2	12.9	3.9	4.4	268,523
9.8	2.3	12.8	13.8	7.7	6.4	7.8	719,026
10.1	1.9	12.4	10.5	6.9	4.4	5.1	371,811
9.3	2.7	14.3	13.7	5.8	3.0	3.6	31,770
5.4	0.6	9.2	2.3	3.5	1.6	1.0	71,051
11.4	2.1	8.5	16.3	5.6	2.1	3.9	29,397
6.8	1.4	17.2	5.0	2.9	2.0	0.7	38,058
4.6	0.9	14.0	6.3	3.0	3.0	1.9	126,945
8.1	1.1	22.2	4.5	3.6	2.2	1.3	46,787
12.0	1.9	14.9	24.2	4.2	4.5	2.6	78,983
14.2	2.5	12.0	14.2	4.6	4.0	3.6	50,191

APPENDIX TABLE 4
Occupation by Ethnic Group, Employed Persons, 1990
(row percentages)

NATIVE BORN	MANAGERS, PROFESSIONALS, AND TECHNICIANS	SALES	CLERICAL	SERVICES	CRAFTS	OPERATIVES
English	59.5	11.9	15.6	6.3	3.3	2.9
German	47.6	11.9	19.4	8.1	6.3	6.1
Irish	38.5	10.6	22.4	12.9	7.3	7.6
Italian	31.1	12.5	25.9	10.4	9.4	9.9
Jewish	54.1	13.7	19.5	5.0	3.6	3.8
Black	14.9	7.6	28.2	22.0	5.6	12.6
Puerto Rican	17.0	10.1	23.7	20.6	8.2	18.6
FOREIGN BORN						
Soviet	33.5	10.5	14.9	14.7	14.1	11.3
Chinese	15.6	8.4	10.0	26.3	6.7	32.5
Indian	41.0	14.5	19.4	8.4	4.7	11.5
Korean	23.8	31.4	10.0	12.6	8.1	13.6
Dominican	10.0	11.8	11.7	22.6	9.3	32.9
Colombian	12.5	8.9	13.3	27.8	11.3	25.7
Jamaican	21.4	7.7	21.1	29.5	9.7	11.8
Guyanese	16.6	10.0	28.2	20.2	9.0	15.1

Source: The 1990 U.S. Census PUMS.

Note: Rows do not add to 100 due to rounding.

APPENDIX TABLE 5
Political Status by Population Group, 1989

Group	Population	Voting-Age Citizens	Registered Voters	Democratic Primary Voters	General Election Voters
Asian	6.7	4.4	3.4	0.9	1.5
Black	25.2	22.8	26.0	34.2	26.8
Latino	24.4	17.9	15.1	12.4	11.5
White	43.2	54.9	55.5	52.5	60.2
Liberal	NA	NA	NA	14.1	17.5
Catholic	NA	NA	NA	20.5	19.7
Outer borough Jewish	NA	NA	NA	13.4	13.5
Protestant and other	NA	NA	NA	4.5	9.5

Sources: Population and Voting-Age Citizens from 1990 U.S. Census PUMS. Registered Voters by Race from NYC Districting Commission. White subgroup figures for registered voters estimated by the NYC Districting Commission. Primary and General election votes for racial groups estimated from ED-level data from NYC Districting Commission; white subgroups estimated using CBS primary and general election exit polls.

Notes: NA stands for not available. Decimal numbers are percentages.

Bibliography

RECENT OVERVIEWS OF NEW YORK CITY

Mollenkopf, John H., and Manuel Castells, eds., *Dual City: Restructuring New York* (New York: Russell Sage Foundation, 1991).

Sassen, Saskia, *The Global City: New York, London, Tokyo* (Princeton, NJ: Princeton University Press, 1992).

CHANGING PATTERNS OF LAND USE

Caro, Robert, *The Power Broker: Robert Moses and the Fall of New York City* (New York: Vintage Books, 1975).

Fainstein, Susan S., and Norman Fainstein, "Governing Regimes and the Political Economy of Redevelopment in New York City," in John H. Mollenkopf, ed., *Power, Culture, and Place* (New York: Russell Sage Foundation, 1989).

Fainstein, Susan S., Norman Fainstein, and Alex Schwartz, "Economic Shifts and Land Use in the Global City: New York, 1940–1987," in Robert A. Beauregard, ed., *Atop the Urban Hierarchy* (Savage, MD: Rowman and Allanheld, 1989).

Hudson, James R., *The Unanticipated City: Loft Conversions in Lower Manhattan* (Amherst: University of Massachusetts Press, 1985).

Marcuse, Peter, "Abandonment, Gentrification, and Displacement: Linkage in New York City," in Neil Smith and P. Williams, eds., *Gentrification of the City* (Winchester, MA: Allen and Unwin, 1986).

Marcuse, Peter, "'Dual City': A Muddy Metaphor for a Quartered City," *International Journal of Urban and Regional Research* 13:4 (December 1989): 697–708.

Mollenkopf, John H., "City Planning," in Charles Brecher and Raymond Horton, eds., *Setting Municipal Priorities, 1990* (New York: New York University Press, 1989).

Savitch, Hank V., *Post-Industrial Cities: Politics and Planning in New York, Paris, and London* (Princeton, NJ: Princeton University Press, 1988).

Stegman, Michael A., *Housing and Vacancy Report, New York City, 1987* (New York: Department of Housing Preservation and Development, City of New York, April 1988).

Stegman, Michael A., *Housing in New York: Study of a City, 1984* (New York: Department of Housing Preservation and Development, City of New York, 1984).

Waldinger, Roger, "Beyond Nostalgia: The Old Neighborhood Revisited," *New York Affairs* 10:1 (1987): 1–13.

Whyte, William Hollingsworth, *The City: Rediscovering the Center* (New York: Doubleday, 1988).

Zukin, Sharon, *Loft Living: Culture and Capital in Urban Change* (Baltimore, MD: Johns Hopkins University Press, 1982).

POVERTY AND THE LABOR MARKET

Bailey, Thomas, and Roger Waldinger, "The Changing Ethnic Division of Labor," in John H. Mollenkopf and Manuel Castells, eds., *Dual City: The Restructuring of New York* (New York: Russell Sage Foundation, 1991).

Rosenberg, Terry J., *Poverty in New York 1980–1985* (New York: Community Service Society, 1987).

Rosenberg, Terry J., *Poverty in New York 1985–1988: The Crisis Continues* (New York: Community Service Society, 1989).

Rosenberg, Terry J., *Poverty in New York City, 1991: A Research Bulletin* (New York: Community Service Society, 1992).

Stafford, Walter W., *Closed Labor Markets: Underrepresentation of Blacks, Hispanics, and Women in New York City's Core Industries* (New York: Community Service Society, 1985).

Stafford, Walter W., with Edwin Dei, *Employment Segmentation in New York City Municipal Agencies* (New York: Community Service Society, 1989).

Sullivan, Mercer L., *Getting Paid: Youth Crime and Work in the Inner City* (Ithaca, NY: Cornell University Press, 1989).

Tobier, Emanuel, *The Changing Face of Poverty: Trends in New York City's Population in Poverty 1960–1990* (New York: Community Service Society of New York, November 1984).

Waldinger, Roger, "Changing Ladders and Musical Chairs: Ethnicity and Opportunity in Post-industrial New York," *Politics and Society* 15:4 (1986–1987): 369–402.

WHITE ETHNIC GROUPS

Bayor, Ronald H., *Neighbors in Conflict: The Irish, Germans, Jews, and Italians of New York City, 1929–1941* (Baltimore, MD: Johns Hopkins University Press, 1978).

Gabaccia, Donna, *From Sicily to Elizabeth Street, Housing and Social Change among Italian Immigrants* (Albany, NY: SUNY Press, 1984).

Gabaccia, Donna, *Militants and Migrants: Rural Sicilians Become American Workers* (New Brunswick, NJ: Rutgers University Press, 1988).

Glazer, Nathan, and Daniel P. Moynihan, *Beyond the Melting Pot: The Negroes, Puerto Ricans, Jews, Italians, and Irish of New York City* (Cambridge, MA: MIT Press, 1963, 1970).

Gurock, Jeffrey, *When Harlem Was Jewish, 1870–1930* (New York: Columbia University Press, 1979).

Landesman, Alter, *Brownsville: The Birth, Development, and Passing of a Jewish Community* (New York: Bloch Publishing, 1969).

Lowenstein, Steven M., *Frankfurt on the Hudson: The German-Jewish Community of Washington Heights* (Detroit, MI: Wayne State University Press, 1989).

Moore, Deborah Dash, *At Home in America: Second Generation New York Jews* (New York: Columbia University Press, 1981).

Rieder, Jonathan, *Canarsie: The Jews and Italians of Brooklyn against Liberalism* (Cambridge, MA: Harvard University Press, 1985).

Rosenwaike, Ira, *A Population History of New York* (Syracuse, NY: Syracuse University Press, 1972).

AFRICAN AMERICANS AND PUERTO RICANS

Baver, Sherrie, "Puerto Rican Politics in New York City: The Post World War II Period," in James Jennings and Monte Rivera, eds., *Puerto Rican Politics in Urban America* (Westport, CT: Greenwood Press, 1984).

Bourgeois, Philippe, "Crack in Spanish Harlem: Culture and Economy in the Inner City," *Anthropology Today* 5:4 (1989): 6–11.

Clark, Kenneth, *Dark Ghetto* (New York: Harper and Row, 1965).

Connelly, Harold X., *A Ghetto Grows in Brooklyn: Bedford Stuyvesant* (New York: New York University Press, 1977).

Osofsky, Gilbert, *Harlem: The Making of a Ghetto: Negro New York, 1890–1930* (New York: Harper and Row, 1971).

Rodriguez, Clara, *Puerto Ricans: Born in the U.S.A.* (New York: Unwyn Hyman, 1989).

Susser, Ida, *Norman Street: Poverty and Politics in an Urban Neighborhood* (New York: Oxford University Press, 1982).

Waldinger, Roger, "Race and Ethnicity," in Charles Brecher and Raymond D. Horton, eds., *Setting Municipal Priorities, 1990* (New York: New York University Press, 1989).

THE NEW IMMIGRANTS

Bailey, Thomas, *Immigrant and Native Workers: Contrasts and Competition* (Boulder, CO: Westview Press, 1987).

Bogen, Elizabeth, *Immigration in New York* (New York: Praeger, 1987).

Boggs, Vernon, Gerald Handel, and Sylvia Fava, eds., *The Apple Sliced* (South Hadley, MA: Bergin and Garvey, 1984).

Foner, Nancy, ed., *New Immigrants in New York* (New York: Columbia University Press, 1987).

Georges, Eugenia, *The Making of a Transnational Community: Migration, Development, and Cultural Change in the Dominican Republic* (New York: Columbia University Press, 1990).

Grasmuck, Sherri, and Pat Pessar, *Between Two Islands: Dominican International Migration* (Berkeley: University of California Press, 1991).

Kasinitz, Philip, *Caribbean New York: Black Immigrants and the Politics of Race* (Ithaca, NY: Cornell University Press, 1992).

Kim, Illsoo, *New Urban Immigrants: The Korean Community in New York* (Princeton, NJ: Princeton University Press, 1981).

Kwong, Peter, *The New Chinatown* (New York: Hill and Wang, 1987).

Laguerre, Michel S., *American Odyssey: Haitians in New York City* (Ithaca, NY: Cornell University Press, 1984).

Leavitt, Roy, and Mary Lutz, *Three Immigrant Groups in New York City in the Human Services: Dominicans, Haitians, Cambodians* (New York: Community Council of Greater New York, 1988).

Papademetriou, Demetrios G., and Nicholas DiMarzio, *Undocumented Aliens in the New York Metropolitan Area* (New York: The Center for Migration Studies of New York, Inc., 1986).

Pencak, William, et al., eds., *Immigration to New York* (Philadelphia, PA: Balch Institute Press; London: Associated University Presses, 1991).

Salvo, Joseph J., et al., *The Newest New Yorkers: An Analysis of Immigration into New York City During the 1980s* (New York: New York City Department of City Planning, 1992).

Waldinger, Roger, *Through the Eye of the Needle: Immigrants and Enterprise in New York's Garment Trades* (New York: New York University Press, 1986).

White, E. B., *Here Is New York* (New York: Harper and Brothers, 1949).

Winnick, Louis, *New People in Old Neighborhoods: The Role of New Immigrants in Rejuvenating New York's Communities* (New York: Russell Sage Foundation, 1990).

Wong, Bernard, *Chinatown: Economic Adaptation and Ethnic Identity of the Chinese* (New York: Holt, Rinehart, and Winston, 1982).

Wong, Bernard, *Patronage, Brokerage, Entrepreneurship, and the Chinese Community of New York* (New York: AMS Press, 1988).

Youssef, Nadia, *The Demographics of Immigration: A Socio-Demographic Profile of the Foreign-Born Population in New York State* (New York: The Center for Migration Studies of New York, Inc., 1992).

POLITICS

Arian, Asher, Arthur Goldberg, John H. Mollenkopf, and Edward Rogowsky, *Changing New York City Politics* (New York: Routledge, 1991).

Bellush, Jewel, and Dick Netzer, eds., *Urban Politics: New York Style* (Armonk, NY: M. E. Sharpe, 1992).

Brecher, Charles, and Raymond D. Horton, "The Public Sector," in John H. Mollenkopf and Manuel Castells, eds., *Dual City: Restructuring New York* (New York: Russell Sage Foundation, 1991).

Brecher, Charles, and Raymond D. Horton with Robert A. Cropf and Dean Michael Mead, *Power Failure: New York City Politics and Policy Since 1960* (New York: Oxford University Press, 1993).

Falcon, Angelo, "Black and Latino Politics in New York City: Race and Ethnicity in a Changing Urban Context," *New Community* 14:3 (Spring 1988): 370–384.

Green, Charles, and Basil Wilson, *The Struggle for Black Empowerment in New York City: Beyond the Politics of Pigmentation* (New York: Praeger, 1989).

Harris, Louis, and Bert Swanson, *Black-Jewish Relations in New York City* (New York: Praeger, 1970).

Haycock, Nancy, *The Nonprofit Sector in New York City* (New York: Nonprofit Coordinating Committee, 1992).

Jennings, James, *Puerto Rican Politics in New York* (Washington, DC: University Press of America, 1977).

Jennings, James, and Monte Rivera, eds., *Puerto Rican Politics in Urban America* (Westport, CT: Greenwood Press, 1984).

Katznelson, Ira, *City Trenches: Urban Politics and the Patterning of Class in the United States* (New York: Pantheon, 1981).

McNickle, Chris, *To Be Mayor of New York: Ethnic Politics in the City* (New York: Columbia University Press, 1993).

Mollenkopf, John H., *A Phoenix in the Ashes: The Rise and Fall of the Koch Coalition in New York City Politics* (Princeton, NJ: Princeton University Press, 1992).

Mollenkopf, John H., "The Postindustrial Transformation of the Political Order in New York City," in John H. Mollenkopf, ed., *Power, Culture, and Place: Essays on New York City* (New York: Russell Sage Foundation, 1988).

Mollenkopf, John H., *The Wagner Atlas: New York City Politics, 1989* (New York: The Robert F. Wagner, Sr., Institute of Urban Public Policy, City University of New York, 1989).

Shefter, Martin, *Political Crisis/Fiscal Crisis: The Collapse and Revival of New York City* (New York: Basic Books, 1985).

Sleeper, Jim, *The Closest of Strangers: Liberalism and the Politics of Race in New York* (New York: W. W. Norton, 1990).

Index

Jews
  ancestries, 20, 22, 26, 27
  Bush (George) supporters, 73
  Dinkins (David) supporters, 82, 86, 87
  Farrell (Herman) supporters, 82
  German ancestry, 26, 27
  Giuliani (Rudolph) supporters, 86
  Hasidic communities, 10, 46
  household income, 48
  Jackson (Jesse) supporters, 82
  Koch (Edward) supporters, 75, 77
  in labor force, 46, 48, 94–96
  Lubavitcher community, 8
  mayoral election (1989), 86, 97
  mayoral primary (1989), 82, 86, 97
  political involvement, 61
  population, 5, 22, 26
  residence patterns, 8, 26
  Russian ancestry, 20, 26
  voter registration, 62, 63, 65, 97
  voting-age citizens, 97

Kew Gardens, 10, 26, 75, 86, 87
Koch, Edward I., 73, 75, 76, 77, 78, 82, 83, 86
Koreans, 20, 34, 35, 36, 37, 94–96

Labor force, 5, 41, 42, 44–49, 93
  employment by ethnic group, 20, 94–95
  employment trends by industry, 92
  occupations by ethnic group, 48, 96
La Guardia, Fiorello, 69
Latin Americans. *See* Latinos; South Americans
Latinos
  AIDS deaths, 49
  Dinkins (David) supporters, 79, 82, 85–86
  drug-related deaths, 49
  Farrell (Herman) supporters, 82
  household income, 17, 19, 41, 43, 49
  Jackson (Jesse) supporters, 77, 78, 82

  Koch (Edward) supporters, 75, 77, 86
  in labor force, 5, 20, 45, 46, 47, 48, 49, 94–96
  mayoral election (1989), 85–86, 97
  mayoral primary (1989), 82, 86, 97
  population, 5, 6, 7, 8, 10, 13, 30, 93
  post-1965 immigration, 5, 19, 20
  presidential election (1988), 73
  residence patterns, 8–9, 10, 19, 27, 30, 41, 49, 86
  voter registration, 62, 63–64, 65, 66, 69, 73, 77, 89, 97
  voting-age citizens, 61, 97
  See also Dominicans; Hispanics; Puerto Ricans; South Americans
Laurelton, 10
Liberal assembly districts, 63, 65, 97
  Dinkins (David) supporters, 79, 82, 86, 87
  Farrell (Herman) supporters, 82
  Jackson (Jesse) supporters, 82
  Koch (Edward) supporters, 77, 86
  mayoral election (1989), 86, 97
  mayoral primary (1989), 86, 97
Liberal party, 61
Lindsay, John V., 69
Little Neck, 10, 73
Low birth-weight babies, 49, 51
Lower East Side, 20, 27, 86
Lubavitcher community, 8

Males. *See* Men
Manhattan, viii, 8, 9, 10, 20, 26, 27, 34, 41, 49, 63, 65, 69, 73, 75, 77, 82, 87
  See also specific neighborhoods and sections
Manhattan Beach, 86
Marine Park, 75
Mayoral election (1989), 86–89, 97
Mayoral primaries (1985), 75, 76, 77, 78, 82–84
Mayoral primaries (1989), 66, 69, 73, 77, 79, 80–81, 82, 83–84, 86–88, 89, 97